Costume

IN THE THEATRE

COSTUME

IN

JAMES LAVER

*A former Keeper of the Victoria
and Albert Museum, London*

THE THEATRE

GEORGE G. HARRAP & CO. LTD

LONDON   TORONTO   WELLINGTON   SYDNEY

First published in Great Britain 1964
by GEORGE G. HARRAP & Co. LTD
182 High Holborn, London, W.C.1

Composed in Baskerville type and printed by Jarrold & Sons Ltd, Norwich
Made in Great Britain

CONTENTS

Acknowledgments	*page*	13
Dressing up to dance		15
Costume in the Greek and Roman Theatre		24
Mysteries, Miracles, and Moralities		39
Pageant and Masque beget Opera and Ballet		58
The Commedia dell'Arte		81
Costume in Shakespeare's Plays		95
Opera and Ballet		140
From Noverre to Diaghilev		164
The Twentieth Century		186
Select Bibliography		220

LIST OF ILLUSTRATIONS

PLATES IN COLOUR

FACING
PAGE

Design for masque costume. Anonymous. Franco-Florentine, early seventeenth century. London, Victoria and Albert Museum ... 16

Design for ballet costume, late seventeenth century, by Jean Bérain. London, Victoria and Albert Museum ... 64

Design for ballet costume, mid-eighteenth century, by Louis-René Boquet. London, Victoria and Albert Museum ... 144

Costume design by Léon Bakst for *The Sleeping Princess*, 1921. London, Victoria and Albert Museum ... 192

PLATES IN MONOCHROME

PAGE

Processional chorus of riders and mimic horses. From an amphora in the Berlin Museum ... 33

Actor dancing. Terra-cotta statuette ... 34

Tragic actor in mask and *cothurnus*. Terra-cotta statuette ... 34

Dancing girl. Tanagra statuette. Attica, fourth century B.C. Berlin Museum ... 35

Pedlar in the Old Comedy. Terra-cotta statuette. Munich ... 35

Character in the Comedy of Menander. Terra-cotta statuette. Oskar Fischel Collection ... 36

Tragic and comic masks. Mosaic. Rome, Capitoline Museum ... 36

Character in the Comedy of Menander. Terra-cotta statuette. Oskar Fischel Collection ... 37

Comedians and masks. Relief. Rome, Lateran Museum ... 37

Scenes from Terence. From manuscript in Bibliothèque Nationale, Paris ... 38

Christ before Pilate. Miniature by Jean Fouquet. Chantilly, Musée Condé ... 53

The Judgment of Paris. Tableau vivant in street theatre. Late fifteenth century ... 53

Christ before Pilate. Sixteenth-century polychrome sculptures. Varallo, Piedmont, Chapel 35 of the Sacro Monte ... 54

Saint George and devils. Scenes in the *Ommeganck*, Brussels, 1615, painting by Denis van Alsloot. London, Victoria and Albert Museum ... 55

Devil masks. Innsbruck, Ferdinandeum ... 56

Pageant costume. Drawing by Leonardo da Vinci, *c.* 1506–7, Windsor Castle. Reproduced by gracious permission of H.M. the Queen ... 69

Two costume designs by Francesco Primaticcio. Stockholm, National Museum ... 70

Two costume designs by Francesco Primaticcio. Stockholm, National Museum ... 71

Two costume designs for opera or ballet. Franco-Florentine, *c.* 1590. London, Victoria and Albert Museum ... 72

PAGE

Costume design for opera or ballet. Franco-Florentine, *c.* 1590. London, Victoria and Albert Museum   73

Design for masquer's costume by Inigo Jones. Chatsworth, Devonshire Collection   74

Design for lady masquer's costume by Inigo Jones. Chatsworth, Devonshire Collection   75

Design for grotesque costume by Inigo Jones. Chatsworth, Devonshire Collection   76

Costume designs for French court ballet. Paris, Louvre   76

Design for grotesque costume by Inigo Jones. Chatsworth, Devonshire Collection   77

Costume design by Stefano della Bella. London, British Museum   78

Costume design by Stefano della Bella. London, British Museum   79

Costume design by Stefano della Bella. London, British Museum

Molière's costume as Sganarelle. Engraving by Simonin   91

Costume of Il Capitano in the Italian Comedy. Engraving by Abraham Bosse   91

Harlequin in the Italian Comedy. Late eighteenth century. London, Victoria and Albert Museum   92

Harlequin costume after Claude Gillot. 1695   92

Pantaloon in the Italian Comedy. Late eighteenth century. London, Victoria and Albert Museum   93

Scaramouche costume after Claude Gillot. 1695   93

Italian Comedy scene. Hôtel de Bourgogne, *c.* 1630. Engraving by Abraham Bosse   94

The Red Bull Theatre, Clerkenwell, *c.* 1672. From F. Kirkman's *The Wits* or *Sport upon Sport*   103

Scene from *Titus Andronicus*. From a manuscript of 1595 in the possession of the Marquess of Bath   103

Quin as Coriolanus, 1749   104

Macbeth and the Witches. From the first illustrated edition of Shakespeare's Works. Edited by Rowe, 1709   104

Costume for Comus, 1757   105

Mr Smith as Alexander in *The Rival Queens*, 1778   106

Mr and Mrs Barry as Jaffier and Belvidera in *Venice Preserv'd*, 1776   106

Mr Garrick and Miss Younge in *Tancred and Sigismunda*, 1776   107

Mr Yates as Malvolio in *Twelfth Night*, 1776   107

Mr Garrick as Macbeth, 1775   108

Mr Macklin as Shylock, 1775   108

Mr Webster as Douglas, 1778   109

Mrs Yates as Electra, 1777   110

Mrs Barry as Phaedra in *Phaedra and Hippolitus*, 1777   111

Miss Younge as Cleopatra in *Antony and Cleopatra*, 1776   112

Mrs Bulkley as Mistress Ford in *The Merry Wives of Windsor*, 1776   112

Miss Brunton and Mr Holman as Palmira and Zophna in *Mahomet*, 1786   113

Edmund Kean as Richard III   114

David Garrick as Richard III. From an engraving after the painting by Hogarth   114

	PAGE
Mrs Hartley as Lady Jane Grey, 1776	115
Mrs Hartley as Jane Shore, 1776	115
Miss Stuart as Joan la Pucelle in *Henry VI, Part 1*, 1786	116
Miss Brunton as Cordelia in *King Lear*, 1785	116
Mrs Pope (formerly Miss Younge) as Cleopatra in *Antony and Cleopatra*, 1786	117
Mrs Wells as Lavinia in *Titus Andronicus*, 1785	117
Mrs Barnes as Anne Bullen in *Henry VIII*, 1786	118
Mrs Kemble as Juliet in *Romeo and Juliet, c.* 1780	118
Mrs Cuyler as Cressida in *Troilus and Cressida*, 1785	119
Miss Farren as Olivia in *Twelfth Night, c.* 1780	119
Mr Wrench as Benedick in *Much Ado About Nothing*, 1814	120
Miss Bolton as Ophelia in *Hamlet*, 1813	121
Mrs W. West as Hermione in *The Winter's Tale*	122
Mrs Warner as Hermione, 1845	123
Mr Young as Hamlet, 1813	124
Miss Smith as Portia in *The Merchant of Venice*, 1813	124
Mr Wallack as Alessandro Massaroni in *The Brigand*, 1830	125
Mr Macready as Shylock	126
Mr Macready as Othello, 1836	126
Mr Macready as Macbeth	127
Mr Macready as King John and Mr Cooper as Hubert	127
Mrs Fitzwilliam as Mistress Page in *The Merry Wives of Windsor*	128
Miss Glyn as Cleopatra	129
Miss Woolgar as Rosalind	130
Mr Charles Kean as Hamlet	130
Miss Vandenhoff as Juliet	131
Miss Glyn as Lady Macbeth	131
Miss Glyn and Mr Hoskins as Isabella and Lucio in *Measure for Measure*	132
Charlotte and Susan Cushman as Romeo and Juliet	133
Mr Phelps as Falstaff, 1846	134
Mr Edmund Kean as Othello	135
Salvini as Othello	136
Ira Aldridge as Othello, 1852	137
Ada Rehan as Rosalind in *As You Like It*	138
Design for ballet costume for Louis XIV by Henri Gissey. London, Victoria and Albert Museum	147
Costume design for the *Carrousel* of 1662 by Henri Gissey. London, Victoria and Albert Museum	148
Design for ballet costume, *c.* 1670. London, Victoria and Albert Museum	148
Design for ballet costume, *c.* 1650. London, Victoria and Albert Museum	149

PAGE

Design for ballet costume, *c.* 1670 by Henri Gissey. London, Victoria and Albert Museum   149

Design for ballet costume, *c.* 1670 by Henri Gissey. London, Victoria and Albert Museum   150

Design for ballet costume, *c.* 1670 by Henri Gissey. London, Victoria and Albert Museum   151

Design for ballet costume, *c.* 1670 by Henri Gissey. London, Victoria and Albert Museum   151

Design for ballet costume, *c.* 1670 by Henry Gissey. London, Victoria and Albert Museum   152

Design for ballet costume, *c.* 1670 by Henri Gissey. London, Victoria and Albert Museum   153

Design for ballet costume, late seventeenth century, by Jean Bérain. London, Victoria and Albert Museum   153

Design for ballet costume, late seventeenth century, attributed to Jean Bérain. London, Victoria and Albert Museum   154

Design for ballet costume, late seventeenth century, by Jean Bérain. London, Victoria and Albert Museum   154

Design for ballet costume, late seventeenth century, by Jean Bérain. London, Victoria and Albert Museum   155

Design for ballet costume, late seventeenth century, by Jean Bérain. London, Victoria and Albert Museum   155

Design for ballet costume, late seventeenth century, by Jean Bérain. London, Victoria and Albert Museum   156

Design for ballet costume, late seventeenth century, by Jean Bérain. London, Victoria and Albert Museum   156

Design for ballet costume, late seventeenth century, by Jean Bérain. London, Victoria and Albert Museum   157

Design for ballet costume, late seventeenth century, by Jean Bérain. London, Victoria and Albert Museum   157

Design for ballet costume, late seventeenth century, by Jean Bérain. London, Victoria and Albert Museum   158

Costume design by Claude Gillot for the *Ballet des Eléments*. Etching by F. Joullain   158

Design for ballet costume, late seventeenth century, by Jean Bérain. London, Victoria and Albert Museum   159

Costume design by Claude Gillot for the *Ballet des Eléments*. Etching by F. Joullain   159

Design for costume by Louis-René Boquet. Paris, Bibliothèque de l'Opéra   160

The Fitzgiggo Riots, showing the stage of Covent Garden Theatre, 1763   160

Design for costume by Louis-René Boquet. Paris, Bibliothèque de l'Opéra   161

Stage setting and costumes by De Vrede at the Schauburg, 1749. Engraving by S. Fokke. Oskar Fischel Collection   161

French ballet costumes, *c.* 1780   162

French ballet costumes, *c.* 1780   162

Costume design by Auguste Garnerey for the ballet *Aladin*. Lithograph by Engelmann   171

Costume design by Auguste Garnerey for the ballet *Aladin*. Lithograph by Engelmann   171

Shepherd's costume in *The Twin Princes*   172

Mlle Noblet in the ballet *Cendrillon*   172

Carlotta Grisi and Jules Perrat in the ballet *La Esméralda*. Lithograph by J. Bouvier   173

PAGE

Zoë Beaupré as Queen Elizabeth, 1831. Drawing by A. E. Chalon. London, Victoria and Albert Museum 174

Joan of Arc. Photograph. London, Victoria and Albert Museum 175

Tristan and Isolde, 1865. Oskar Fischel Collection 176

Mlle Bréval of the Paris Opéra as Brunnhilde, 1908 177

Ballet costume, *c.* 1860 178

Ballet costume, *c.* 1850 178

Ballet costume, *c.* 1885 178

Ballet costume, *c.* 1890 178

Ballet costume, *c.* 1860 179

Ballet girl 'off duty', *c.* 1840 179

Music Hall costume, *c.* 1890 180

Music Hall costume, *c.* 1870 180

A ballet in progress. *Punch*, 1879 180

Music Hall costume, *c.* 1870 181

Music Hall costume, *c.* 1890 181

Robinson Crusoe, *c.* 1880 182

Costumes for Man Friday and Mrs Crusoe in the pantomime *Robinson Crusoe* by C. Wilhelm, 1882. London, Victoria and Albert Museum 182

The Sisters Levey in their Ostrich Dance, 1894. From *The Sketch* 183

Miss St Cyr, 1894. From *The Sketch* 184

Costume design by Alexandre Benois for Nijinsky in *Armide*, St Petersburg, 1907. London, Victoria and Albert Museum 203

Costume design by Léon Bakst for le Bouffon Russe in *The Sleeping Princess*, 1921. London, Victoria and Albert Museum 204

Costume design for Anna Pavlova by Natalia Gontcharova. London, Victoria and Albert Museum 204

Costume design for ballet by Andreenko, 1925. London, Victoria and Albert Museum 205

Costume design for ballet by Andreenko, 1925. London, Victoria and Albert Museum 205

Costume design by Norman Wilkinson 'of Four Oaks' for *A Midsummer Night's Dream*. London, Victoria and Albert Museum 206

Costume design by Claud Lovat Fraser for *La Serva Padrona*, 1919. London, Victoria and Albert Museum 207

Costume design by Charles Ricketts for Hermione in *The Winter's Tale*. London, Victoria and Albert Museum 208

Costume design by Charles Ricketts for Leontes in *The Winter's Tale*. London, Victoria and Albert Museum 209

Costume design by Doris Zinkeisen for *The Insect Play*, 1923. London, Victoria and Albert Museum 210

Costume design by Simon Lissim for *La Prochaine*, 1937. London, Victoria and Albert Museum 210

PAGE

Costume design by Ernst Stern for *Le Bourgeois Gentilhomme*, 1912. London, Victoria and
Albert Museum   211

Costume design by Michael Weight for *The Importance of Being Earnest*, 1930. London,
Victoria and Albert Museum   .   212

Costume design by George Sheringham for *The Duenna*, 1924. London, Victoria and
Albert Museum   213

Costume design by Alexandra Exter. London, Victoria and Albert Museum   214

Costume design by Alexandra Exter. London, Victoria and Albert Museum   214

Two costume designs by Jean-Victor Hugo for *Roméo et Juliette*   215

Costume design by E. Prampolini for *La Nuit Métallique*. London, Victoria and Albert
Museum   215

Two dancers in the ballet *Tempo Universel*, Monte Carlo, 1959. *Figaro*, photo: Jacques
Normand   216

Performance of Romain Rolland's *Carnaval* at the Russian Propaganda Theatre   216

Costumes for ballet by Oskar Schlemmer. Oskar Fischel Collection   217

Costume in Handel's *Julius Caesar*, Darmstadt, 1927. Photo: Hermann Collman   217

Costumes for ballet by Oskar Schlemmer. Oskar Fischel Collection   218

ACKNOWLEDGMENTS

I wish to make the following acknowledgments for illustrations used in this book. To H.M. the Queen for her gracious permission to use the drawing by Leonardo on page 69, to the Marquess of Bath for the illustration on page 103, to the Trustees of the Chatsworth Settlement for the four designs in the Devonshire Collection at Chatsworth on pages 74 to 77, and to *Punch* for the cartoon on page 180.

I am also grateful to the following museums and collections for granting me permission to reproduce items in their possession: Berlin, the Staatliche Museen (pages 33 and 35); Chantilly, the Musée Condé (53); Innsbruck, the Ferdinandeum (56); London, the British Museum (78, 79, 80); the Mansell Collection (36, 37, 54, 76, 91); Munich, the Glyptothek und Museum Antiker Kleinkunst (35); Paris, the Bibliothèque Nationale (38); and the Bibliothèque et Musée de l'Opéra (160, 161); and Stockholm, the Nationalmuseum (70, 71).

Finally, I acknowledge my indebtedness to the Victoria and Albert Museum for supplying almost all the prints and photographs and for permission to reproduce those items in its collection.

CHAPTER ONE

DRESSING UP TO DANCE

IN modern parlance we make a sharp division between 'theatrical' and 'ordinary' clothes. We even distinguish between plays that are dressed in contemporary clothes and those dressed in the clothes of people of other times and places. We refer to the latter as 'costume plays.' We have the same distinction in mind when we go to a 'costumier' to choose something to wear at a fancy-dress ball. We think we know the difference between 'dressing' and 'dressing up.' It is only when we begin to study the history of costume in general that all these distinctions begin to be rather blurred.

So soon as clothes are anything more than a mere device of decency or a protection against the weather they inevitably assume a dramatic quality of some kind. When a mayor puts on his robes he is both putting on 'historical' costume and assuming a character. The legal gentleman who covers his bald head with a full-bottomed wig and his subfusc suit with the judicial scarlet is getting ready to 'play the part' of a judge. It would not be far off the mark to say that all clothes for special occasions and stylized clothes of any kind are, in effect, theatrical costume. We are at least on safe ground in suggesting that *in origin* all clothes are theatrical costume. Certainly primitive man would have understood this well enough. For him the putting on of clothes at all was a dramatic gesture. Even when he wore no clothes in ordinary life he was in the habit of 'dressing up to dance.' The history of theatrical costume is much longer than the history of theatrical décor. It goes back to the very beginning of mankind.

Perhaps it goes back even further, for Wolfgang Köhler has described a dance of chimpanzees, in which the animals moved in a ring, beat time with one paw, pirouetted, and went through all the movements of a primitive dance. He continues: "Pour les danses de ce genre, le chimpanzé aime à s'orner d'objets divers et surtout de fils, de plantes grimpantes, de chiffons qui pendillent et s'agitent."[1] What is this but 'dressing up to dance'? Theatrical costume is older than man himself.

The chimpanzees were presumably doing this for pure pleasure, and there is no doubt that this element figured largely in the dances of primitive man. There is delight in rhythmical movement, as every child knows; there is also pleasure in imitation. Primitive man imitates the movements of animals and birds and the swaying of trees, and by so doing enters into *rapport* with them, becomes one with them, and, since they influence him, he begins to think that he can influence them, by what the anthropologists call 'sympathetic magic.' This notion is by no means extinct even to-day. One has only to watch the spectators at a boxing bout to see that every blow the champion delivers is reinforced by a hundred mimetic blows in the audience. At a football match the fans can hardly restrain themselves from kicking in the direction of the goal.

Mimetic magic is more effective if more than one person takes part in it. Emotionally the crowd is greater than the sum of its parts. The whole tribe makes in unison the same instinctive gesture; inevitably the gesture becomes rhythmical, becomes a dance, and in doing so is doubly effective. The dance, says Hambly, "produces a condition in which the unity, harmony and concord of the community are at a maximum."[2] Early man regarded dancing as indispensable at all the crises of life. Primitive religion was essentially something "to be danced out."

But even before we reach the stage of religion—in the sense of a system of belief about the gods—we find tribal dancing to induce the

[1] Wolfgang Köhler, *The Mentality of Apes* (London, 1925).
[2] W. D. Hambly, *Tribal Dancing and Social Development* (London, 1926).

Design for masque costume. Anonymous
Franco-Florentine, early seventeenth century

game to appear, the rain to fall, and the cattle and women to breed. But imitation does not stop at gesture, or even at posture (the Australian aboriginal imitating the stance and leap of the kangaroo). Primitive man tried to resemble as closely as possible the animal he wished to influence. He did this by flaying the victim of a previous chase and clothing himself in the skin. He 'got into the skin of his part,' as we would say. He would have liked to get inside the animal's head too, but primitive man was not an expert taxidermist, so he carved a head out of wood or bark and inserted his own head into it. In a word, he invented the mask.

"Among the Mandan Indians," says Tylor,

> when the hunters failed to find the buffaloes on which the tribe depended for food, every man brought out of his lodge the mask of a buffalo's head and horns, with the tail hanging down behind, which he kept for such an emergency, and they all set to 'dance buffalo.' Ten or fifteen masked dancers at a time formed the ring, drumming and rattling, chanting and yelling; when one was tired he went through the pantomime of being shot with bow and arrow, skinned and cut up; while another, who stood ready with his buffalo head on, took his place in the dance. So it would go on, without stopping day or night, sometimes for two or three weeks, till at last these persevering efforts to bring the buffalo succeeded, and a herd came in sight on the prairie.[1]

Loomis Havemeyer tells us that the natives of Torres Strait wear before a hunting or fishing expedition masks of tortoise-shell. "The form of the mask is supposed to have much to do with the success of an undertaking, and so before a hunting trip they will wear only the mask of an animal and before a fishing trip that of a fish."[2]

He also reminds us of the religious nature of these ceremonies and that "the men who take part are, for the time being at least, almost priests of the animals which they are portraying."

This is an example of an ambivalence that the primitive accepts quite naturally. The animal is at once his victim and his best friend, and the emotion of joy at the conclusion of a successful chase is balanced by a feeling of guilt. So the element of propitiation enters into the magical

[1] Sir E. B. Tylor, *Anthropology*, pp. 296–297.
[2] Loomis Havemeyer, *The Drama of Savage Peoples* (Oxford, 1916).

drama, for drama it is as soon as men begin to dress up and assume a character not their own.

We must not forget that the animal hunted was often the totem animal of the tribe, and looked upon, therefore, as the present incarnation of a mythical ancestor. This ancestor was an animal, but also, in a mystical sense, a man; so the mask of the ancestor is no longer merely an animal. On the contrary, we find all kinds of combinations: bird-men, kangaroo-men, monkey-men. The way was open to the creative imagination. It is to this original duality, says Jean-Louis Bédouin,[1] that the mask owes its most powerful effects. There is mimicry in it, but there is also symbolism.

The need for propitiation is also felt in relation to immediate ancestors, and this gives rise to the widespread phenomenon of the 'ghost dance.' The assumption of the characters of other *men* is another step forward in theatrical activity. It opens the door to *story* as opposed to mere mimetic gesture: the myth begins to emerge from the rite. Appropriate costumes are necessary, and, remarks Raglan, "it is hardly an exaggeration to say that nowhere in the world is anyone allowed to take a prominent part in any ritual unless he is dressed for it."[2]

In this dressing up the mask played an important—indeed, an overwhelmingly important—part; in the studying of theatrical costume there is no escape from it. The mask, says Gregor, is

a world phenomenon exempt from time and space, as the first and strangest utterance of a universal religious feeling . . . far older than myth or saga or any other more developed form. . . . Poised on the mask are all the terrible experiences and fancies of mankind. . . . Beasts lord it over us. Mouths gape. Frightful eyes stare at us from every side. Since man began to shape and carve these things, he has freed himself little by little. When he laid the finishing touch to his mask and invented the theatre, he mastered his own myth instead of letting himself be mastered by it. At its height the mask stands for the plenitude of creative power, that is yet aware of the secret of its source. Here in our hand we hold one of the most effective keys to the secret realm of our own past.[3]

[1] Jean-Louis Bédouin, *Les Masques* (Paris, 1961).
[2] Lord Raglan, *The Hero* (London, 1936).
[3] Joseph Gregor, *Masks of the World* (London, 1936–37).

Within recent years anthropologists and other scholars have begun to take an increasing interest in the mask. In Antwerp in 1956 there was an elaborate exhibition in which every kind of mask was displayed: some five hundred examples from every part of the world. What struck the visitor was their essential similarity, in spite of differences in style and technique. We know that in archaic Greece there were initiation ceremonies for the young men in which masked dancers played a part. We know that the masks used were, for the most part, hideous, grimacing, intended to strike terror. The ceremonies still held among primitive peoples in Africa are of the same character. In this respect, remarks Bédouin, "the distance between an African fetishist and a worshipper of Dionysus only appears to be great because we ourselves have ceased to participate in the world of magic in which they move."[1]

When the hunting stage was succeeded by the pastoral stage there must have been an interruption in the development of 'drama.' Shepherds and herdsmen are solitary beings. It was necessary that the pastoral phase should give place to agriculture before play-acting, even in its most primitive sense, could move forward again. When it did so it laid down almost from the first the lines of all subsequent theatrical development. It was still magical; its object was still to ensure the food supplies of the community, no longer by persuading animals to come and be killed, but by persuading the corn to grow.

Perhaps the threshing-floor was the first localized 'theatre'; although this is a problem for the historians of theatre architecture and stage décor. We are concerned with the costumes, and here it seems that there was less innovation than might have been expected. We still find the masks and animal disguises of the hunters in the rituals of the agriculturists.

It was long before the gods assumed human shape, and even when they did so traces of their animal ancestry can still be found. Sometimes, as in ancient Egypt, they retained their animal-heads—*e.g.*, the ibis-head of Thoth, the God of Wisdom—and even in classical Greece the gods were accompanied by the symbolical animals whose form they once wore. Zeus has his eagle and Venus her doves. Dodona means

[1] Bédouin, *op. cit.*

"Dove-woman," and Eckenstein has pointed out the frequent "associa-tion of a woman bearing an animal name with a cult-centre. . . . At Delphi there was a Pythia, or Snake Woman; at Elis there was the Tragia, or Goat Woman."[1] The very word 'tragedy' is derived from 'goat,' although the scholars are still arguing about the precise signi-ficance of this. It is enough for our present inquiry to note the strange persistence in the theatre of the most primitive costume elements of ritual drama. In the sanctuary of Demeter and Persephone at Lycosura, in Arcadia, there is a carving of semi-human, semi-animal figures dancing and playing musical instruments. The bodies are those of women, but the heads, paws, and feet are those of horses, asses, pigs, cats, and hares. "It is reasonable to suppose," says Sir James Frazer, "that these dancing figures represent a ritual dance which was actually performed in the rites of Demeter and Persephone by masked men and women, who personated the goddesses in their character of beasts."[2]

But in the drama of agricultural peoples we find something new: the emergence of the 'Divine King,' who summed up in himself the fertility hopes of his people. In primitive times the crops were considered safe as long as the king enjoyed health and vigour. When he began to grow old and feeble he was killed and replaced. Originally he was probably killed and replaced every year, and the accompanying ceremonies constituted a ritual drama staggering in its consequences, both for the history of religion and for the history of the theatre.

As civilization advanced the actual slaying of the Divine King was transformed into a mimic murder. The same man died and rose again, just as the grain of wheat did when the Old Year was replaced by the New Year. It is strange that the last scattered fragments of this drama persisted almost until our own day, when the Mummers' Play and the Sword Dance could still be seen in English villages. Both were derived from the mock slaying of the fertility god. Its influence on the Greek plays that have come down to us needs no stressing.

Until comparatively recent years historians of the theatre have passed at a bound from the dances of primitive peoples to the drama of ancient

---

[1] L. Eckenstein, *A Spell of Words* (London, 1932).
[2] Sir James Frazer, *Spirits of the Corn and of the Wild* (London, 1912), vol. ii, p. 339.

Greece. Yet Herodotus, writing in 449 B.C., makes mention of two Egyptian plays dealing with the Passion of Osiris. We know that such plays were performed, notably at Abydos, from very ancient times. No text has survived, but we have the account of an eyewitness and participant dating from 1868 B.C. This is contained in the inscription in hieroglyphic on the Stele of Ikhernofret, now in Berlin. Ikhernofret was sent to Abydos to build a new shrine to Osiris and to regulate the ceremonies of his cult. These seem to have taken the form of a procession, a water-pageant, and a sham fight (realistic enough, however, for many of the actor-warriors to die of their wounds). Unfortunately, however, the stele contains no representation of the performers, so that we can only guess at the costumes worn. It is probable that, as the principal parts in the drama were performed by priests, these wore their vestments, just as the Christian priests did in the early medieval plays. Animal masks may have been worn by some of the enemies of the god, a suggestion made more probable by the fact that so many of the Egyptian deities were animal-headed.

Another incised slab known as the Shabaka Stone, now in the British Museum, describes a coronation festival play dating back to about 3000 B.C., although the stone itself was cut in the eighth century B.C. Once again there are no pictures that tell us what the actors wore. However, there is an extant text of the coronation drama dating from the reign of Sesostris I, the second king of the Twelfth Dynasty, who ascended the throne about 1970 B.C. This is a real drama, consisting of forty-six scenes, with dialogue between two or more *dramatis personae*, interspersed with stage directions.

Fortunately, the great Harvest Festival which was celebrated all over Egypt is depicted in detail in the temple of Rameses III at Medinet Habu,[1] and we are able to study the clothes worn by those taking part. These are, in general, the clothes familiar to us from Egyptian wall-paintings, but many of the celebrants wear two feathers in their hair, and a wall-carving at Denderah actually shows the construction of the animal-head masks worn by the priests.

Less is known of Babylonian myth and ritual, but one text has

---

[1] G. Wilkinson, *Manners and Customs of the Ancient Egyptians*, vol. iii, Pl. LX.

survived. It was copied in the Seleucid period from a record of the seventh century B.C., the original of which may be of even earlier date. We have only one tablet of many which, altogether, described the "rites of the prerogative of Anu, the holy offices, the ceremonies of kingship, the divine offices . . . the proceedings of the enchanters, the conjurers, the singers and the craftsmen, all who are in the company of the foreman, not counting all that pertains to the students of divination."

Religious festivals in Babylonia centred about the figure of Dumu-zi, or Tammuz; and Tammuz was undoubtedly a god of grain who died and rose again. The festival of Akitu in his honour is supposed to have been held at the New Year, and lasted for eleven days. It is plain that the ceremonies that took place must have been similar in general outline to those held in Egypt in honour of Osiris. The costumes worn have to be deduced from seals and processional friezes in Nineveh.

There is at Boghazkeui, in Cappadocia, a rock-carving that represents a Hittite religious procession. "The figures on the left hand are almost exclusively men, while those on the right are all women. The men all wear the cone-shaped Hittite cap and tip-tilted shoes, and they are performing a running-step dance, the right feet being partly raised, and touching the ground only with their toes. The inscription belongs approximately to B.C. 1200."[1]

That the Jews in ancient times had anything that might be called 'theatrical costume' would probably be denied by many; and, indeed, we have very little direct evidence apart from such casual Biblical references as the statement that "David danced before the Lord." Of recent years, however, scholars have come increasingly to believe that, in the days before the Exile, there was not so much difference between Hebrew practices and those of their neighbours, even in matters of religion, as had formerly been supposed. A scholar of the standing of F. J. Hollis, for example, has put forward the theory that the Temple of Jerusalem, as built by Solomon, was orientated in the same way as the sun-temples of Egypt.[2] An examination of the Jewish festivals leads

[1] W. O. E. Oesterley, *The Sacred Dance* (Cambridge, 1923).

[2] In *Myth and Ritual*, edited by S. H. Hooke (Oxford, 1933): "The Sun-Cult and the Temple at Jerusalem," by F. J. Hollis, p. 111.

to the conclusion that the Feast of Tabernacles was originally adopted from the Babylonian Akitu festival, and that many of the Psalms that have come down to us were originally part of a processional litany. It has been suggested that the 'tabernacles,' or 'booths,' represented the sacred grove in which a sacred marriage was celebrated between Jahweh and his consort Anath.[1] All mention of this consort has been eliminated from the sacred records during the post-Exilic period, when the Jewish religion became uncompromisingly monotheistic. "We have," says T. H. Robinson,

> from outside our Bible one very important piece of evidence bearing on this subject. The temple at Elephanté contained, in the fifth century, not only Jahweh, but also several subordinate deities. These included the goddess Anath, whose name is clearly to be connected with the place-names Anathoth and Beth-Anath. These show that she was carried by the Jewish immigrants from Palestine into Egypt with Jahweh. . . . It is difficult to avoid the conclusion that rites, similar to those found elsewhere, were observed in pre-exilic Israel and that these included a recital or representation of the annual marriage of Jahweh and Anath.[2]

If this is so, then Israel shared in the culture-patterns of Egypt and Babylon to a degree hitherto unrecognized, and the costumes worn in its dramatic-religious celebrations probably showed a blending of the two influences.

When all is said, however, there is a long step between ritual drama, even if it involves the impersonation of the god, and true theatre, with its impersonations of human characters. This vital step was taken by the Greeks, who, beginning in primitive times with 'dressing up to dance,' progressed to the masterpieces of Aeschylus, Sophocles, and Euripides. It is this development we must now consider.

[1] *Ibid.*, "Early Hebrew Festival Rituals," by W. O. E. Oesterley, p. 136.
[2] *Ibid.*, "Hebrew Myths," by T. H. Robinson, p. 185.

CHAPTER TWO

COSTUME IN THE GREEK AND ROMAN THEATRE

IT is now fairly generally agreed that the Greek drama arose out of the choric dances performed in honour of Dionysus.[1] This Asiatic god, hardly mentioned by Homer, made his way through Phrygia and Thrace about the beginning of the eighth century B.C., his cult following the progress of viniculture throughout the whole of Greece. The wild revels of his devotees gradually became refined into choric dances. The origin of the word 'dithyramb' is much disputed, but there is no doubt that it was connected from the earliest times with the worship of Dionysus, and that his priests improvised chants in his honour, accompanied by flute and lyre. The half-mythical Arion is said to have introduced it at Corinth, where it became mingled with the worship of Pan and his train of satyrs.

Dionysus was himself the god of vegetation, and therefore of rebirth. Processions in his honour were necessarily phallephoric, images of the organs of generation being carried in triumph. Wild orgies followed, and such are frequently represented in vase-painting, with the participants disguised as satyrs and maenads. An Attic vase of the fifth century B.C. preserved in the Museum at Naples shows very clearly the costumes worn in the satyr play.

---

[1] There are, however, rival theories. They are listed—and dismissed—by Margarete Bieber, *The History of the Greek and Roman Theater* (Princeton, 1939).

Dionysus and Ariadne recline beneath a spreading vine. Next to them are three heroes clad in the solemn robes of tragedy, with the masks of Herakles, Laomedon the King of Troy, and his daughter Hesione. A chorus of satyrs with their leader, old Papa-Silenus in his shaggy goatskin, the poet Demetrios, the celebrated flutist Pronomos and a lyrist are assembled about them. The satyrs wear goatskin loin cloths with tails attached; only the leaders of the semi-choruses are distinguished by a chiton and a loin cloth of woven fabric.[1]

In earlier vases the satyrs have horses' tails attached to their bodies, which are otherwise quite nude.

A considerable number of Greek vases show men dressed as animals. An amphora in Berlin carries a picture of a processional chorus of mimic horses, the men acting these being clothed with skins and bearing horses' heads; a sixth-century oenochoe in the British Museum has bird-figures with wings and feathers. In both of these the structure of the costumes is quite easily seen.

We are here, of course, in the presence of a very primitive form of dressing up, and it is interesting that the convention of animal disguises should have persisted into the work of as sophisticated a writer as Aristophanes. So much is indicated by the very names of his plays: the *Wasps*, the *Birds*, the *Frogs*; and even in the *Clouds* we know from literary records that the actors wore bird-like masks. But we are hurrying on too fast.

A large body of material has now been accumulated, chiefly through the work of German scholars, concerning the costumes of what is called the Dorian mime, a kind of performance which arose at Megara in the sixth century B.C. before its development as the Old Comedy in Athens. The Louvre possesses a series of Corinthian vases depicting dancing figures. "Many of the scenes," says Allardyce Nicoll, "might be nothing but imaginative conceptions of grotesque Dionysiac revelry or pictures of real-life festivity wholly unconnected with the theatre, but several indications are given to us that some at least of these vases do reproduce scenes of a theatrical kind."[2] One of the vases shows Dionysus being robbed of a wine-jar by his slaves, and Nicoll points out that the

[1] Bieber, *op. cit.*, p. 15.
[2] Allardyce Nicoll, *Masks, Mimes, and Miracles* (London, 1931), p. 21.

costumes worn are very similar to those depicted on a black-figured Corinthian amphora now at Athens and dating from the beginning of the sixth century. The costume consists of a tight-fitting vest, either plain or spotted, and padded buttocks. The phallus is exposed, and in some cases is of such enormous dimensions that it could not have been other than artificial.

This device, so strange to modern notions of propriety, long persisted in comedy, as, after prolonged controversy, most scholars seem now to agree. In earlier modern books it was often suppressed in the illustrations, thereby, as F. M. Cornford rightly complains, falsifying the evidence. The same authority sums up the matter as follows:

> Aristophanes' professed renunciation of this article of costume seems to imply definitely that it was familiar on the Attic stage, and that the public were getting tired of jokes about it. His professions must not be taken too seriously, for not only does he in the extant plays use all the other 'vulgar devices' which he condemns, but the use of the phallus itself seems to me certain in the case of some of his own characters. The probable conclusion seems to be that it had been a traditional part of the actor's dress . . . and that Aristophanes, and perhaps Eupolis too, were trying to get rid of it, but did not altogether succeed. No doubt it was still popular with the less refined part of their audience and it had behind it a religious tradition.[1]

There is, at all events, no doubt of its prominence in the costumes worn by the Dorian mimes. In Athens itself early Dionysiac vases show the god attended, not by slaves but by satyrs, but the slave costume soon established itself, as can be gathered from the evidence of vase-painting and from small terra-cotta statuettes. One of these (a double figure), now at Würzburg, shows an old man in a long robe, and with a padded stomach, talking with a slave in a short tunic showing the pendent phallus. A figurine of the fourth century B.C. now in the Louvre is that of a comic actor in an identical costume, but in this case he wears a mask. A fourth-century Attic vase at Leningrad actually shows actors holding masks in their hands. Costumes and masks very similar are to be seen on vases representing the Phlyakes, the mimes performed in the city of Tarentum, in Southern Italy.

That the costumes of the Old Comedy and of the mimes should show

---

[1] Francis Macdonald Cornford, *The Origin of Attic Comedy* (London, 1914), p. 183.

a derivation from Dionysian revels is, perhaps, hardly surprising; but the cult of the wine-god gave rise also to Athenian tragedy and some of the noblest works of the human imagination. We cannot here pause to consider all the problems involved; it is enough to note that the costumes worn by the actors in tragedy were extremely proper and dignified. They seem to have been fully established by the time of Aeschylus and to have persisted unchanged for centuries. They consisted of the long *chiton*, a loose garment extending from the throat to the ankles, but differing from the *chiton* of ordinary life in having sleeves (considered effeminate by the Athenians) and in being coloured and patterned (the ordinary *chiton* being uncoloured and plain). In addition to the *chiton*, a *himation* (long cloak) or *chlamus* (short cloak) was worn. Stage cloaks too were brightly patterned and coloured, the colours being selected, it is surmised, for their symbolic effect, queens wearing purple and mourners black.

The most characteristic feature of Greek tragic costume was the *cothurnus*, or thick-soled boot, worn to give more height to the actor, appearing as he did before so large an audience, and to indicate the differing degrees of dignity in the personages. Thus kings were made taller than their companions, and this effect was reinforced by the increased height of the *onkos*, a kind of lofty head-dress forming part of the mask. The bodies of the actors were padded to prevent these devices from making them seem excessively slim.

The mask was an essential part of the costume and the element which makes the Greek tragic theatre so different from that of later times. Although it was derived from long tradition, its immediate purpose, like that of the *cothurnus*, was a practical one. In a huge amphitheatre facial expression would have been lost on all but a few of the spectators seated in the front rows. The mask also served, by its structure, as a kind of megaphone, the amplification of the voice being necessary in spite of the excellent acoustics of Greek theatres. The masks, which were made of linen, cork, or wood, carefully carved and painted, served also to indicate the age of the person represented.

Pollux, in his *Onomastikon*, enumerates some thirty of the masks used in tragedy: the mask of extreme old age, for such characters as Priam;

the 'white' or not so old man with white hair and a thick white beard;
the grey-haired man; the 'tyrant' with thick black hair and beard; the
fair and ruddy-complexioned man, and one fair but pale to indicate
sorrow or sickness; and a whole series of young men and youths. Other
masks were those of the 'rustic,' the boastful soldier, and the parasite.
A whole class of masks was provided for lower-class characters such as
servants: the faithful old serving-man, the 'chief slave,' the 'crisp slave,'
the Greek cook, the foreign cook, etc.

Some seventeen female masks are enumerated, beginning with three
old hags: the thin old woman, the fat old woman, and the coarse-faced
old servant (the lower classes are consistently given snub noses), with
all but four of her teeth missing. After these comes a series of young
women's masks: two matrons, one virgin, and two 'false virgins'—that
is, young girls who have been kidnapped or suffered other undeserved
misfortunes—a bawd, a 'mistress,' or kept woman, an 'accomplished
courtesan,' three younger courtesans, a lady's maid, and a confidante
of the courtesan. All these masks served the purpose of allowing a
character to be recognized as soon as it appeared on the stage.

It was once thought that the long-sleeved robe worn by the tragic
actors had been derived from the robe worn by the priests of the
Eleusinian cult. Margarete Bieber has shown, however, that "it was
not . . . the actors who borrowed their dress from the Eleusinian priests,
but rather the Eleusinian priests who borrowed this costume from the
actors."[1] And she is able to point to a black-figured vase of an early
date in Bonn that depicts Dionysus in the sleeved robe. The truth seems
to be that the Bacchic revelries gave rise both to tragedy and comedy,
and to the Eleusinian Mysteries themselves.[2]

An important series of terra-cotta statuettes found in a single grave
in Athens is now in the Metropolitan Museum of New York. They
represent characters in the Middle Comedy (380–330 B.C.), but still
have the costumes of the Old Comedy. The personages are probably
not all from one play, but they show quite clearly that characterization
had already proceeded to the stage of recognizable stock figures.

In the New Comedy of Philemon and Menander the chorus had

---

[1] Bieber, *op. cit.*, p. 38.   [2] L. R. Farnell, *Cults of the Greek States* (Oxford, 1907).

declined in importance, the surviving elements of the old phallic procession had faded away, the old indecent costume was abandoned and the dress of everyday life substituted. Pollux (who lived much later, in the reign of the Emperor Commodus) gives a list of the masks of comedy as well as those of tragedy. There were dignified old men, brave young men, the 'man with the pointed beard' who was always a villain, and several varieties of parasite. There were seven kinds of slaves, including an aged freedman, and two cooks, one bald and one with brown hair. There was a similar number of female masks, including no less than seven different types of courtesan. Attempts were sometimes made to change the expression of a character by making one half of the mask show a smiling and the other a frowning face.

The masks of the 'straight' characters show an increasingly naturalistic tendency. On the other hand, the masks of countrymen and slaves, with coarse, exaggerated features, were carried on almost unchanged from former times. The slaves' masks even continued to show features of the early fifth century B.C., as if to demonstrate how very archaic they were. Cooks' masks were, by tradition, particularly grotesque, having been carried over unchanged from the old Dorian mime.

The importance of the mime has only recently begun to be recognized. Aristotle knew of four kinds of drama—the tragic, the comic, the satyric, and the mime. It seems certain that

> in Sparta, in Megara, and in other near-by centres had grown up a type of play, which, non-choral and therefore distinguished from Attic comedy, not only influenced the Athenian theatre, but provided the basis for the further development of the mime. This farcical play introduced grotesquely clad stock figures, most of them wearing the phallus, who presented scenes of real life alongside mythological burlesque. In all, probably, most of the dialogue was improvised, and perhaps the performances had become professional by the fifth century B.C.[1]

The phrase "mythological burlesque" gives us pause, yet it is certain that popular entertainment in ancient Greece was very much concerned with presenting parodies of those themes which the Greek tragedians had raised to such heights of poetry and grandeur. Such scenes were played not only in Greece itself but in the Greek colonies that had

[1] Allardyce Nicoll, *Masks, Mimes, and Miracles.*

established themselves in Sicily and in Southern Italy, chiefly in the area of what is now Naples. Fortunately, a mass of information has been unearthed concerning the Phlyakes (or 'gossips'), a name applied both to plays and to players. Vase-painters, of one of whom the name —Anteas—has been preserved, decorated their work with scenes from these farces of the fourth century B.C. A favourite *comic* hero was Herakles, and Odysseus runs him close in popularity. Both are shown in a series of ludicrous situations. Zeus himself is not spared; we even find him climbing step-ladders to visit his mistresses. Gods and heroes wear masks indistinguishable from those of the old men in scenes from ordinary life.

From a study of the vases preserved in London, Leningrad, and Berlin it is possible to distinguish three types of 'old men' masks—a snub-nosed, clean-shaven type with a prominent chin, a hook-nosed type with a straggling white beard, and a type without any exaggerated characteristics. Of the middle-aged types one has a short, bristling beard and moustache, and one is clean-shaven. There are various kinds of slave masks, some with wide mouths and some with one eyebrow raised. Peasants are also represented, and examples have been found of masks that bear a startling resemblance to the medieval fool. The costumes worn either suggested nudity by means of tights or consisted of an indecently short *chiton*, the dangling phallus exposed.

In 272 B.C. the Romans captured Tarentum, the centre of Greek civilization in Italy, but if this was a political victory for Rome it was a cultural victory for the Greeks. Half a century later Livius Andronicus was translating into Latin the tragedies of Sophocles and Euripides, and Greek comedy was soon made accessible to Roman audiences. Roman tragedy, when it arose, was a mere imitation of the Greek, the costumes being carried over from one to the other, and although Roman comedy had its own development it need not detain us here. It is sufficient to note that the actors were, at first, unmasked but provided with wigs.

The Romans already had their own crude, popular entertainments, and after the arrival in Rome, in 364 B.C., of Etruscan *ludiones*, dancers and flute-players, the two combined to produce the *satura* or *fabulae saturae*, little scenes of daily life that proved immensely popular.

The new Greek influence gave rise to what are known as the *fabulae*

Atellanae, the name being derived from the town of Atella, in Campania, near to Capua. These rustic farces bear a close resemblance in characterization and costumes to the Phlyakes, and when they were transplanted to Rome they were played by young men of good family who did not lose their civil and military rank by appearing on the stage and who never took off their masks before the public as professional actors were accustomed to do. Professional actors, indeed, were forbidden to appear in the *fabulae Atellanae.*

The masks were those of fixed characters or stock figures, of which four are of particular interest. These are the bragging and greedy Maccus, the stupid Bucco, the foolish old miser Pappus, who is for ever being robbed of his gold and his girl, and the mischievous Dossenus. There were also several thieving slaves and a few non-human characters such as Manducus the ogre and the ghoul Lamia, the latter a frightful spook who pretended to swallow naughty children and afterwards had them cut out of her body.

Professor Nicoll treats Dossenus-Manducus as a single character. With a wealth of classical references he points out that *manducari* means 'to be chewed' and that Manducus has something to do with eating or being eaten. Dossenus, on the other hand, is derived from *dorsum,* meaning 'hump-backed.' Terra-cotta masks have been preserved showing a jutting chin, with open mouth and savage-looking teeth, and a hooked nose, and there is a statuette in the Louvre showing the whole figure with its protruding belly and what seems to be a hump. On the immense nose of this figure is a large wart. A bronze found near Cologne shows this same wart, but on the brow. Dr Bieber reproduces a number of masks and remarks: "Characteristic are the crooked face, gigantic nose, puckered corners of a mouth much too broad, unsymmetrical eyebrows and bare forehead. Often there is a wart on the forehead, a Campanian malady (*morbus Campanus*) which frequently occurs in the home of the Atellan farce. Horace mentions a horn-like growth on the forehead of an Oscan juggler."[1] The interesting thing in all this is that the figure we have been describing has lasted, if only in the form of a puppet, until our own day. We call it—Punch.

[1] Bieber, *op. cit.,* p. 416.

Pappus is almost equally interesting. He is plainly derived from Pappos, in the Phlyakes, and it would seem, in spite of the doubts of such scholars as Miclascevsky, that he is clearly the forerunner of Pantaloon in the *commedia dell'arte*. Dr Bieber lends the weight of her authority to belief in the survival of the *Atellanae* throughout the Dark Ages and the medieval period into her own time.

Performances of the Atellan farces were given both in public theatres and in private houses. A valuable reference in Aelius Spartianus' life of Hadrian tells us that the Emperor "often brought forward at his banquets tragedies, comedies, Atellanae, harp-players, readers, and poets, just as suited the occasion." In other words, sometimes he presented a play, sometimes (perhaps for the 'tired businessmen' of his acquaintance) he 'put on a cabaret.' There was no novelty in this. Even in the classical period in Greece banquets were generally concluded, even in the best houses, with performances resembling those of the modern strip-tease clubs of Paris and London. It is true that some of them were supposed to teach a moral lesson, or at least to emphasize the advantages of marriage. In *The Banquet* Xenophon gives us a description of the miming on such an occasion of the loves of Bacchus and Ariadne. It is implied that those taking part wore few clothes or none. Female dancers, jugglers, and acrobats were represented on Greek vases either naked or wearing coloured drawers with the breasts bare.

It was the Romans who expanded this kind of performance into a public spectacle. The feasts in honour of the goddess Flora included an entertainment resembling those at the Folies-Bergère and similar theatres. A favourite subject was the Judgment of Paris, and the Emperor Elagabalus himself once appeared in such a scene, playing the part of Venus! In *The Golden Ass* Apuleius has left us a description of a similar performance of the Judgment of Paris, Juno and Minerva being dressed in the modest garb of the Roman matron and unmarried girl respectively, Venus in a wisp of blue silk tissue. Perhaps it is not surprising that the early Christians lumped all theatrical performances together in a common anathema.

Processional chorus of riders and mimic horses
From an amphora in the Berlin Museum

Actor dancing

Tragic actor in mask and cothurnus

Terra-cotta statuettes

Tanagra statuette of dancing girl
Attica, fourth century B.C.

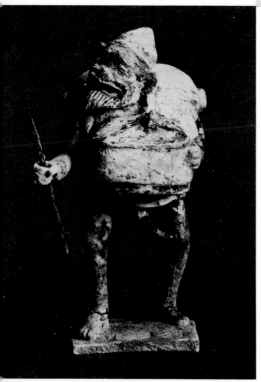

A pedlar in the Old Comedy
Terra-cotta statuette

35

*Statuette of a character in
the Comedy of Menander*

Roman mosaic of tragic and comic m[...]

Statuette of a character in
the Comedy of Menander

Roman relief of comedians and masks

Manuscript illustrations
of scenes from Terence

CHAPTER THREE

MYSTERIES, MIRACLES, AND MORALITIES

FROM the first the Christian Church was hostile to the theatre, or, at least, to what the theatre had become in the Roman world. Tertullian in his treatise *De Spectaculis*, written in the closing years of the second century, declares:

> The theatre is especially the shrine of Venus. . . . We are commanded to love no immodesty . . . therefore we are cut off from the theatre . . . which is the private council-chamber of immodesty, wherein nothing is approved save that which elsewhere is disapproved. . . . The very harlots also, the victims of the public lust, are brought forward on the stage. . . . Blush the Senate! Blush all ranks! let the very women, the destroyers of their own modesty, shudder at their doings before the light and the public. . . . What manner of thing is it to go from the Church of God to the Church of the Devil? from the sky (as they say) to the stage? . . . Thou must hate, Christian, those things, the inventors whereof thou canst not but hate.[1]

These sentiments were to be echoed with increasing vehemence by Christian writers for the next four centuries. Baptism was refused to anyone who had been a *scaenicus* ('actor') or *scaenica* ('actress'). The astonishing thing is that, while the serious theatre had indeed fallen into decay, the mimes—that is, the theatre at its lowest—continued for a long time even under the Christian emperors. It is interesting to note that it was the Emperor Justinian who made it obligatory for

[1] *Of Public Shows*, translated by the Rev. C. Dodgson, 1842.

dancing-girls, mimes, and acrobats to wear drawers, or at least a *cache-sexe*, although, as the sixth-century writer Procopius declares, Justinian's wife, the Empress Theodora, who had been a dancing-girl herself, was before her elevation in the habit of appearing on the stage without either.

It was the Barbarian invasions that finally brought the mimes to an end as a public spectacle. At Rome, as Allardyce Nicoll tells us, "after the coming of the Lombards in 568 we hear no more of *spectacula* or of theatres. . . . It is undeniable . . . that during the sixth century in Italy and during the seventh century at Constantinople theatrical shows as a whole completely disappear."[1]

He goes on, however, to examine the evidence for the persistence of wandering entertainers, *jongleurs*, and musicians who performed in hall and castle. "Some," says a writer of the early fourteenth century, "transform and transfigure their bodies with indecent dance and gesture, now indecently unclothing themselves, now putting on horrible masks." Such performers have been thought to provide the link between the Roman mimes and the *commedia dell'arte* of the sixteenth century. But this problem must be dealt with at a later stage.

Jongleurs and the like were, however, mere 'cabaret.' True drama had to be born again, and just as the original drama of the Greeks had sprung from the ceremonies in honour of Dionysus, so the drama was born again out of the cult of that other Saviour-God whose worship now covered nearly the whole of Europe. And just as the earlier theatrical development had been the result of an infiltration of legendary stories into the ceremonies in honour of the god, so the whole process repeated itself, and the central drama of Christianity—the daily sacrifice at the altar—threw out offshoots which finally took root and were able to develop with a life of their own. The first sacred dramas were attempts to illustrate Christian doctrine by representing incidents from the life of Christ. The first actors were priests, the costumes were the vestments of the Church, and the theatre was the Church itself.

The liturgical drama was, in its origin, no more than a variant or slight expansion of the liturgy. Although the Mass is essentially

[1] Allardyce Nicoll, *The Development of the Theatre* (fourth edition, London, 1958), p. 60.

dramatic, there is, in its strict form, no *impersonation*, which is generally agreed to be the criterion of drama as such. Yet, in the ancient rite of the church at Lyons, the priest, after the Elevation of the Host, stood for a moment with his arms extended, thus figuring Christ on the Cross. At an early date, also, on Palm Sunday, the story of the Passion was read by several priests, the grave voice of Christ replying to the shrill clamour of the Jews.

The most ancient liturgical drama of which we have any record appeared towards the end of the tenth century. This was the *Drama of the Resurrection* and the *Book of Customs*, attributed to St Dunstan and written for the English monasteries in A.D. 967, describes it in detail:

> It began on Good Friday. On that day, after the veneration of the Cross, it was wrapped in a veil symbolising Christ's shroud and was carried solemnly to the tomb. . . . On the altar there had been prepared an imitation of the tomb [*quaedam assimilatio sepulcri*]. The cross was placed in it and left there until the morning of Easter Sunday. Before the first bells were sounded it was secretly taken away, leaving only the veil in the sepulchre. Then the Mass began and the Gospel for Easter Day was acted before the eyes of the faithful. A monk, clothed in a white alb, seated himself, like the angel, near the tomb. Three other monks, enveloped in long robes which made them resemble women, advanced slowly and as if hesitating with censers in their hands. "Whom seek ye?" asked the angel in a low and gentle voice. "Jesus of Nazareth," replied the holy women. "He Whom ye seek," replied the angel, "is not here. He is risen. Come and see the place where He was laid." He then showed them where the cross had been placed and where there was now only a shroud. Then the holy women took the cloth and held it up for the faithful to see, singing with joy, "The Lord is risen!" At this signal the faithful burst into a song of triumph and all the bells rang out.

We have here, although still within the strict limits of the words of Scripture, impersonation, dialogue, and dramatic action—in short, drama. The emotional effect must have been considerable, and Émile Mâle thought it probable that, from Carolingian times, a similar play must have been enacted in French monasteries also.

One very beautiful early mystery play may be taken as an example of the heights to which the purely liturgical drama could rise. Down one aisle of the church moved a small group of clergy representing the disciples on the road to Emmaus; down another walked a solitary figure representing the risen Christ. They met at the door of the church, exchanged greetings, and walked together, conversing, up the central aisle of the church to the high altar, which represented, by a symbolism as happy as it was expressive, the inn and supper table at Emmaus. "And he was known to them in the breaking of bread."[1]

In this connexion there is an interesting example of the influence of the liturgical drama upon the other arts, notably that of church sculpture. This influence began at a surprisingly early date. It has now been shown that the scene of the pilgrims to Emmaus is reflected in three figures on one of the columns of the cloister of the church of St Trophime at Arles. There can be no doubt, says Émile Mâle, that "the three statues at Arles represent Christ and the pilgrims and that they represent them in the costumes they wore when they acted, in the church, the liturgical drama of the Walk to Emmaus."[2] Even more striking is the sculpture in the church of St Gilles of the scene of the Three Marys buying perfumes on their way to the Tomb. This incident is unknown to Scripture, but it appears in a manuscript preserved at Tours of what must be one of the earliest mysteries, played in Latin on Easter morning.

As early as the eleventh century an expansion of the Easter trope *Quem quaeritis* gave rise to a Christmas play of *The Shepherds*. A trope was an amplification of a passage in the authorized liturgy, and once the principle was admitted the way was open for further developments. The play of *The Shepherds* arose in connexion with the Christmas Mass, but was transferred to Matins, which allowed for a further expansion. The shepherds were clad in the ordinary rural costume of the time, and there was therefore nothing 'theatrical' in their appearance. It was far otherwise with the Three Kings. The Bible speaks only of Wise Men, but "by the fifth century the Magi had become oriental monarchs, were established as three in number, and were assigned various names of which Melchior, King of Tarsus, Caspar, King of Arabia, and Balthazar, King of Saba, were the most frequent designations. . . .

[1] Émile Mâle, "Le Drame liturgique et l'iconographie de la Résurrection" (*La Revue de l'Art*).
[2] Émile Mâle, "Les Influences du drame liturgique sur la sculpture romane" (*La Revue de l'Art*).

These Kings from their earliest appearance in the drama are always costumed formally and magnificently and became favourite subjects of pictorial art."[1] Their appearance in late medieval mysteries is therefore well documented and will be dealt with later. In the early versions, still within the framework of the liturgy, the Three Kings were represented by three of the inferior clergy, wearing copes and crowns. They met before the main altar, upon which, behind a curtain, were the figures of the Mother and Child, surmounted by a star-shaped cluster of lights. They were greeted by two clerics in dalmatics who drew aside the curtain. The Kings adored the Child and then fell asleep. They were roused by a choirboy, dressed in an alb to represent an angel, who warned them not to reveal the whereabouts of the Child to Herod. It will be noted that, with the exception of the Magi's crowns, the costumes worn were still ecclesiastical vestments.

Herod himself could obviously not long be excluded from the story, and, indeed, there is an eleventh-century text from Nevers in which he is introduced. But Herod could not be clothed in ecclesiastical vestments, and his rage at the escape of the Child could not with propriety be played in a church. This is a fact of considerable importance in the development of the mysteries.

It is usual to distinguish between mystery plays—*i.e.*, plays of incidents in Scripture and arising directly from the liturgy—and miracle plays, treating of the lives and martyrdoms of saints. As Hardin Craig points out, however,[2] it is impossible to maintain an absolute distinction between, for example, the liturgical plays of St Nicholas and those of St Thomas and St Paul. Plays concerned with the lives of non-Scriptural saints appear quite early, although we have no texts in England of any other than those concerned with St Nicholas and played inside the church. Similar performances are known to have taken place in France and at Hildesheim early in the twelfth century. Although the text has not been preserved, we know that a play of St Catherine was performed at Dunstable at the end of the eleventh century. It was, however, presented in the school, and the schoolmaster borrowed a number of

[1] Hardin Craig, *English Religious Drama of the Middle Ages* (Oxford, 1955), p. 51.
[2] Craig, *op. cit.*

copes from St Alban's Abbey, an interesting example of ecclesiastical vestments still being used, although the play itself had moved outside the church.

Not only saints but prophets soon began to take their place in the medieval drama. Sermons aimed at the conversion of the Jews had long dwelt on those figures of the Old Testament who had prophesied the Coming of Christ. It was but a step to bring them to life, and a *Prophetae* of the thirteenth century from the cathedral of Laon shows that Isaiah was bearded and clad in a dalmatic, that Moses carried the Tables of the Law, and that Daniel was a splendidly dressed youth. What altered the whole character of what was originally a solemn procession was the inclusion of Balaam, for Balaam, as everybody knew, pronounced his prophecy while seated upon an ass.

Records exist of the performance in the eleventh century, at Limoges, of *The Mystery of the Prophets of Christ*. In this Balaam was not included; but, as Gayley points out, "As soon as the prophets of Christ's coming stepped out of the sermon into a ceremonial procession, Balaam slipped into the throng . . . and where Balaam marched, his ass marched under him."[1] A manuscript that has survived from the early thirteenth century and is now in the British Museum tells us what happened in the ceremony that came to be known as the Feast of the Ass. At the first Vespers the cantor, standing in the middle of the nave, intoned, in Latin: "Let no sour-faced person stay within the church . . . let all be cheerful who would celebrate the *Festa Asinaria*." Every one then went to the west door to welcome the ass, waiting outside, and the animal was conducted up the aisle by the censers, each holding a bottle of wine and a glass. There was drinking, genuflecting, and chanting, the subdeacons and secular clergy braying in chorus. There seem to have been no special costumes for this ceremony, the clergy wearing the usual vestments.

It was far otherwise with the Feast of Fools, with which the Feast of the Ass came to be amalgamated. On New Year's Eve, when the verse in the Magnificat was reached "He hath put down the mighty from their seat," it was interpreted in the most literal manner. The

[1] Charles Mills Gayley, *Plays of our Forefathers* (London, 1909), p. 34.

precentor handed over his staff of office to the subdeacons and the inferior clergy took over, changing places and probably vestments with the canons, sitting in their stalls, censing the altar with black puddings and sausages, performing a burlesque of the Mass, and chanting a drinking song as they marched out of the church. Some of the participants wore motley costumes.

Such practices were more prevalent in France and Germany than in England, and various efforts were made to suppress them. Yet as late as 1445 the Theological Faculty of the University of Paris thought it necessary to issue a letter to the bishops calling upon them to put down "an execrable custom permitted in certain churches, by which the Feast of the Circumcision is defiled. . . . Priests and clerks may be seen wearing masks and monstrous visages at the hours of office. They dance in the choir dressed as women, panders, and minstrels."

The mention of masks is interesting as it provides yet another link between the medieval Feast of Fools and the festival of the Roman Kalends, which took place at exactly the same time of year. In this too the mighty were put down from their seat; there were disguisings and maskings, exchange of clothes, dressing up as animals, and general ribaldry. The parallel serves to remind us how thin was the crust of Christianity over the pagan impulses below, even in the Ages of Faith.

Like other elements of the medieval drama, the Fool gradually became secularized, moving outside the church to form those *confréries des fous* which in the fifteenth century wandered all over France, playing interludes and ribald farces. This brought the medieval fool yet more into line with the Roman mime; even his clothes bore a close resemblance, and, indeed, retained elements of a still more primitive character. The hood worn might have asses' ears, recalling the days when men had worn animal-heads. Or it might be red in colour and surmounted by a crest in the form of a cockscomb. His garments were particoloured, often of red and yellow (the Prologue to Shakespeare's *Henry VIII* mentions a fool wearing "a long motley coat guarded with yellow"), and provided with one huge sleeve, which served as a bag. He carried a bauble that was sometimes in the shape of a phallus with the small head of a fool, a cock, or an ass, with bells attached. All these had a phallic significance,[1] as had also the bladder with rattling peas inside.

The resurgence of the comic element was exemplified in yet another character of the medieval drama. The early mysteries have a beauty and propriety that make them very suitable for performance in a church. Unfortunately, the Devil was not slow to enter in—in a quite literal sense. It was natural that he should have a part to play in many scenes from Scripture, but he very soon showed a tendency to run away with the show. He became, in short, a comic character, and his popularity is attested by all the evidence that has come down to us of his appearance and accoutrements.

The medieval dramatists introduced devils even when they were not needed. They were present at the Nativity and at the Massacre of the Innocents.

> When John the Baptist is seized they raise their exultant cries. A prologue by a demon introduces *The Council of the Jews* in the *Ludus Coventriae*, and a festive scene in Hell accompanies Herod's feast. Then at the Passion it is the devils who inspire Judas, both to betray Christ and to commit suicide. So anxious were the dramatists to make use of this material that they even made the Devil responsible for the dream of Pilate's wife, which ought to have been a divine dispensation. After this follows the diablerie of *The Harrowing of Hell*, of *The Coming of Antichrist*, and of *Doomsday*. Obviously the devils were dear to the medieval imagination, and dear not because of their evil, but because of their comic irresponsibility, their posturings, their extravagance.[2]

The costumes varied within narrow limits. "Men disguised, or partly disguised as animals," says Raglan, "have been, from the earliest times of which we have any knowledge, familiar figures in ritual. . . . We have good reason to believe that a devil was originally a man ritually disguised as a goat, and an angel was originally a boy ritually disguised as a bird."[3] Sometimes, therefore, the Devil was shown covered with hair, as if to demonstrate his lineal descent from the ancient satyrs; sometimes he wore leather, sometimes black cloth, or a mixture of black and

---

[1] L. Eckenstein, *A Spell of Words* (London, 1932), p. 204.
[2] Allardyce Nicoll, *Masks, Mimes, and Miracles*, p. 187.
[3] Lord Raglan, *The Hero*, p. 262.

red to suggest the flames of hell. Sometimes he was covered with feathers, but this seems to have been unusual.

An interesting if somewhat moth-eaten example of the black cloth costume is still preserved in the Ferdinandeum at Innsbruck, as is also an important collection of devil masks. Some of these are horned and some have animal snouts, and terrifying they look. There can be little doubt that they resemble very closely the usual masks of the medieval devils, and none at all, surprising as it may seem, that in the Middle Ages they caused more hilarity than terror. Almost from the beginning, the part of the Devil seems to have been 'played for laughs.'

Even more surprising is the fact that Herod gradually became a comic character. His rage at the escape of the infant Saviour in *The Massacre of the Innocents* was purposely exaggerated, so much so as to give rise to Shakespeare's remark about "out-Heroding Herod." Comic also, although to a lesser degree, was Pilate, and by the end of the fifteenth century these two characters had become the principals. We learn from Sharp's collection of accounts for the craft-plays of Coventry[1] that, while the actor who played God was paid two shillings and Judas eighteenpence, Herod received three-and-fourpence, and Pilate four shillings.

Between 1449 and 1585 the Smiths' Company of Coventry paid out in different years: "for six skins of white leather for God's garment, 18*d.*; for making of the same garment, 10*d.*; for mending a cheverel [peruke] for God, and for sewing of God's coat of leather . . . 12*d.*; for a girdle for God, 3*d.*; for a new sudere [the veronica] for God [*i.e.*, Christ], 7*d.*; for painting the falchion and Herod's face, 10*d.*; for mending of Herod's head, and a mitre and other things, 2*s.*" We learn from the same records that Pilate always had a green coat—at least at Coventry. In the Chester plays Herod had a helmet and painted visor or mask and a gown of blue satin. The Devil (for once) wore feathers, but "all ragged and rent." The winged angels were clad in albs and suits of gold skins. God and His angels continued to wear ecclesiastical vestments.

[1] Thomas Sharp, *A Dissertation on the Pageants or Dramatic Mysteries anciently performed at Coventry* (Coventry, 1825).

Much ink has been spilt on the question of whether Adam and Eve, and the damned souls being prodded by the devils in the direction of hell-mouth, actually appeared on the stage naked or were provided with close-fitting garments of white leather. The latter theory would appear more probable. The miracle plays, with their representations of the martyrdom of the saints, frequently required the victim to be naked—at least in appearance. We know, however, that at Metz in 1468, in a play about the martyrdom of St Barbara, the part of the saint was taken by a young man in a *maillot* with artificial breasts of cardboard, which were chopped off at the required moment.[1]

David Rogers, writing in the early years of the seventeenth century, gives us a list, unfortunately incomplete, of some of the costumes and accessories required for one of the last of the medieval plays produced in England, the "pagiente" at Chester in 1565:

> A cote & hosen wt a bagg & capp for dolor, stayned.
> 2 cotes & a payre hosen for Eve, stayned.
> A cote & hosen for Adam, steyned [*sic*].
> A cote wt hosen & tayle for ye serpente, steyned, wt a wt heare.
> A cote of yellow buck-ram wt ye Grocers' arms for ye Pendon bearer.
> A face & heare for ye Father.
> 2 Hearys for Adam & Eve.[2]

From this it is plain that Adam and Eve not only wore wigs ('hearys'), but coats and hose—Eve even had two coats.

The morality plays that arose at the end of the fourteenth century were not, like the mystery and the miracle plays, concerned with incidents from Scripture or from the lives of the saints. Morality personages were abstractions: Mercy, Peace, Understanding, Perseverance, Repentance, and the Seven Deadly Sins. It must, one feels, have been a tedious *genre*, yet one masterpiece, *Everyman*, has proved within recent years that it can still be revived with effect.

A somewhat similar play, *The Castle of Perseverance*, is thought to have been staged at Lincoln about the year 1425, and a manuscript now in

[1] G. J. Witkowski and L. Nass, *Le Nu au Théâtre* (Paris, 1909), p. 41.
[2] David Rogers, *Breavarye* (1609). The list is reprinted by Sir E. K. Chambers, *The Elizabethan Stage* (Oxford, 1923).

the Folger Shakespeare Library in Washington actually shows us a plan of the stage.[1] This is circular and of the greatest interest, but the notes on costume beneath the drawing do not give us much information.

Indeed, we should be at a sad loss both for descriptions and for illustrations of the costumes worn in medieval drama but for the undoubted reaction between the plays and pictorial art. We have already referred to the sculptures at Arles which represent some of the figures in early liturgical drama. Towards the end of the medieval period, notably in the fifteenth century, such correspondences multiply, even if their exact significance has been the subject of much learned controversy.

Scholars have noted in the religious art of the fifteenth century a new influence, almost a new iconography, which they attribute to the influence of the mysteries; and the mysteries themselves were transformed from about 1400 by the addition of a whole series of new episodes. Up to that date the authors of such pieces had drawn their material either from the Gospels themselves or from the *Golden Legend*. Suddenly there is an enrichment of episodes, and this enrichment Émile Mâle traces to a book entitled *Meditations on the Life of Jesus Christ*, attributed to St Bonaventura.[2] In this work there is a dispute in Heaven between Mercy and Peace on the one side and Justice and Truth on the other, all four represented as "daughters of God." Not only does this scene begin to appear in mysteries played in France, Italy, Spain, and England, but one of the French authors notes in the margin of his text that he has based himself on the *Meditations*.

It was to the *Meditations* that the mysteries owed the increasingly popular scene of the farewell of Jesus to His Mother before going up to Jerusalem; also the scene of the Virgin holding the dead Christ on her knees at the foot of the Cross. This episode, unknown to Scripture, but adopted eagerly by the mysteries, gave rise to innumerable Pietàs in sculpture and pictorial art. In fact, much of the iconography of painters, sculptors, illuminators, and designers of tapestries was inspired by

[1] Reproduced in the Early English Text Society edition of the play, edited by F. J. Furnivall and A. W. Pollard (1904).
[2] Émile Mâle, *L'Art religieux de la fin du Moyen Age en France* (Paris, 1908), p. 13.

themes that were undoubtedly being played on the mystery stages *at the same time*. From this it seems legitimate to conclude that the costumes depicted in art and the costumes worn in actual performances must have resembled one another closely. If this is so, then we are justified in drawing upon all the arts for evidence of fifteenth-century stage costume.

Some have thought that the mysteries borrowed from pictorial art and not vice versa, but this view is strongly contested by Mâle, who gives an impressive list of the modifications in pictures of God the Father, the Virgin, angels, etc., during the fifteenth century that can only be explained by a theatrical origin.

> The extraordinary costumes in which the artists of the fifteenth century clothed the Prophets are theatrical costumes. Jeremiah and Ezekiel who, in the fourteenth century, wore merely a simple tunic and the little Jewish bonnet, are now provided with high hats with turned-back brims loaded with strings of pearls. They have rich furs, girdles of goldsmiths' work, tasselled purses. So bizarre an accoutrement, differing from the current mode, could only have been imagined for a solemn procession or a 'show.'[1]

Formerly God the Father was represented bareheaded and clothed in a simple tunic.

> Everything changes towards the end of the fourteenth century, when painters began to depict what they had seen with their own eyes. . . . How could a poor actor convey the idea of omnipotence? He had no other way of giving himself some kind of majesty than by accumulating all the emblems of human sovereignty— crowns, double crowns, triple crowns. He appeared therefore on the scaffold which figured Paradise, sometimes with the Emperor's crown, sometimes with the Pope's tiara. . . . Thus was born the God-Pope or God-Emperor of the fifteenth century, represented most perfectly in the paintings of Van Eyck. His God, blazing with jewels, has at the same time the tiara of the Pope and the crystal and gold sceptre of the Emperor.[2]

Émile Mâle made a thorough search for indications of such influences. He notes, for example, that in late-fifteenth-century art in France the Virgin and St John, instead of kneeling in adoration of the risen Lord, are provided with chairs. And in the stage directions for the only

[1] Émile Mâle, *op. cit.*, p. 57.   [2] Émile Mâle, *op. cit.*, p. 55.

mystery of the Last Judgment preserved in France[1] are the words, "there must be provided a well-appointed throne for Our Lady to sit beside her Son." "It is clear," says Mâle, "that the actors playing the parts of the Virgin and St John could not have remained kneeling for the three or four hours which the drama lasted."[2] He thinks that this is a plain case of pictorial art being influenced by actual performances of the mysteries.

Sometimes an actual connexion can be traced. The so-called Tour de Beurre of Rouen Cathedral, built in the Flamboyant style and decorated with a large number of statues, is particularly interesting for the study of stage costume. For it is known that there was played at Rouen in 1474 a *Mystery of Octavian and the Sibyl*, embodying the legend that the Emperor Augustus was informed by the prophetess of the birth of Christ. Fainting at the news, the Emperor is supported by the two principal officers of his household, his *sénéchal* and his *connétable*. Now these two figures have been identified in two of the statues that adorn the east face of the Tour de Beurre. But, indeed, the whole statuary of the tower might be described as a mystery turned into stone. Here are Moses, Adam and Eve, David, sibyls, prophets—all the favourite characters of the mystery plays.[3]

Information as to the costuming of the plays can be obtained from contemporary tapestries and also, most profitably, from fifteenth-century altar-pieces. These, with their "simultaneous settings" and crowds of figures in fantastic attire, have been aptly named *rétables-guignols*,[4] and probably came closest to representing the staging and costumes of the late medieval drama. These conclusions are supported by the one actual fifteenth-century representation of a mystery play that has come down to us. This is the famous miniature by Fouquet in the illuminated manuscript known as *Les très riches Heures du Duc de Berry*, reproduced in the present volume (p. 53).

Perhaps we cannot do better to conclude a section dealing with the

---

[1] A. Jeanroy and H. Teulié, *Mystères provençaux du XVe siècle* (Toulouse, 1893).

[2] Émile Mâle, *op. cit.*, p. 499.

[3] Louise Lefrançois-Pillion, "Le 'Mystère d'Octavien et la Sibylle' dans les statues de la Tour de Beurre à la Cathédrale de Rouen" (*La Revue de l'Art*, lxvii, 1925), p. 145.

[4] By Jacques Mesnil in *L'Italia e l'Arte Straniera* (Rome, 1922).

costume of medieval drama than to draw attention to pictures of the *Ommeganck* (now preserved in the Victoria and Albert Museum) in spite of the fact that they were painted, not in the Middle Ages, but early in the seventeenth century. *Ommeganck* means simply 'procession,' and it took place every year in Brussels under the patronage of Notre-Dame du Sablon, a church founded in 1213 by the influential Guild of Crossbowmen. The annual procession was instituted at least as early as 1359, and nearly a hundred years later it was witnessed by the French Dauphin who afterwards became King Louis XI.

The procession, which was ostensibly in honour of the translation of a miraculous image of the Virgin from Antwerp to Brussels, included all the clergy and religious Orders as well as the magistrates of the city, but it was essentially a procession of the guilds, of which there were no less than fifty-four. In addition there was a series of symbolical cars, some of which give a very good idea of the method of staging on movable cars so much practised in the mystery cycles. Unfortunately we have no picture of these dating from the medieval period, but the Spanish Netherlands undoubtedly preserved, even in the early seventeenth century, elements which had long vanished from pageants elsewhere, and therefore even in the pictures of the *Ommeganck* of 1615 which is the one with which we are dealing, we find elements that had probably changed very little from the representations of a hundred or a hundred and fifty years earlier.

Two of the cars in particular stand out, for one represents the Annunciation and the other the Nativity. The former is a charming tableau, with obvious resemblances to certain paintings of the same subject by Rogier van der Weyden. The angel wears a long white robe and is furnished with white wings; the Virgin wears a crown and contemporary costume (for the medieval equivalent we must, of course, take away her ruff), and she kneels at a *prie-dieu*. The Nativity car is more elaborate. Under a thatched roof we see, in addition to the Virgin and Child, St Joseph and the shepherds, as well as the ox and the ass.

Even more important, from our point of view, are the devils who act as marshals of the procession and are obviously conceived as comic characters. The Chief Devil is engaged in a fight with St Michael (here

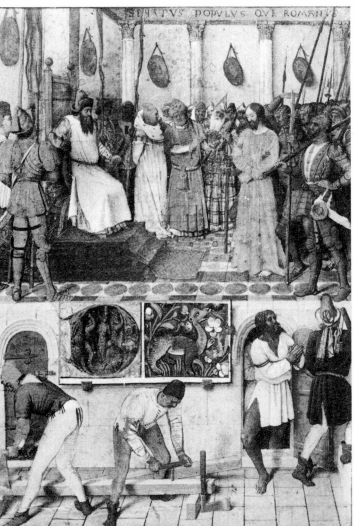

Christ before Pilate
Miniature by Jean Fouquet

Tableau vivant: The Judgment of Paris
Street theatre: late fifteenth century

Christ before Pilate
Sixteenth-century polychrome sculptures

Scenes in the Ommeganck, *Brussels, 1615*
RIGHT *St George and the Devil*
BELOW *Devils*

Devil masks used in medieval German Passion plays

again we must make a costume adjustment and take away his trunk-hose, but otherwise he is in the medieval angelic tradition). The Devil wears trousers with bat-like flaps to accentuate his diabolic mien, and he bears in the middle of his back another face. The Devil in medieval art is almost always double-faced, or even poly-faced, with additional visages on his belly, on his knees, and even on his posterior. The inferior devils also wear trousers with bat-like appendages, and one has the face of a bird. All these costumes are of particular interest as they undoubtedly derive from a long tradition of devilry as depicted on the medieval stage.

The other cars need not concern us here as they depict subjects such as the Court of Diana and Apollo, and the Muses. The gradual preponderance of such subjects over Biblical themes as the Middle Ages yielded to Renaissance influences must be the theme of our next chapter.

CHAPTER FOUR

PAGEANT AND MASQUE BEGET OPERA AND BALLET

THROUGHOUT the Middle Ages there had been a precarious balance between Church and State. On the whole the Church had weighed more heavily, but in the fifteenth century the weight began to be thrown into the other scale. The new centralized monarchies, dukedoms, and other principalities began to chafe at the restrictions of their power by a Universal Church, and men's thoughts turned back to the last great secular State of which they had any knowledge— the Roman Empire. The ancient world was rediscovered, its monuments and statues brought to light, and the figures of the old mythology ceased to be the 'devils' they had appeared to the medieval imagination and became once more gods and goddesses in their own right.

The first impact of Renaissance ideas can be noted surprisingly early, mythological figures appearing at the elaborate Court banquets of the late medieval period. Max von Boehn makes the odd but convincing remark that "opera arose out of table decoration."

> In the fifteenth century table appointments, thanks to the example set by the Burgundian court, became ultra-magnificent in style. The banquets given by Duke Philip the Good, once as a spur to the organization of a crusade, at another time to celebrate the marriage of his son, Charles the Bold, with Margaret of York, were long remembered for their eccentric table-decorations. They took the form of a stage-setting, and so well were the *mise-en-scène* and the feast combined that it

was not possible to tell where the one left off and the other began. The table appointments, or, more correctly speaking, the living pictures, included Paris with the three goddesses vying for the apple. . . . A pie was served up in which was concealed an orchestra of twenty-eight musicians; a whale sixty feet long appeared, from whose wide-open jaws poured sea-gods and sirens, who proceeded to dance a quadrille. . . . This was a favourite style of entertainment in Italy too. At the nuptials of Galeazzo Sforza and Isabella of Aragon in Milan the banquet was a dramatic performance, the serving being arranged as a ballet with as many scenes as there were courses to the meal. Mercury came on with a stolen calf, Diana with a stag, Orpheus brought birds, Theseus the Calydonian boar, Vertumnus fruit, and Hebe the wine, while around them frolicked, with song and dance, shepherds, satyrs, Silenuses, and other mythological folk. The best artists used to lend their services; Leonardo da Vinci, for instance, made the mechanical devices required on these occasions.[1]

Leonardo also designed costumes for such entertainments; one of his drawings for what seems to be a shepherd is preserved in the Library of Windsor Castle, and is reproduced in the present volume (p. 69).

These were, so to speak, *private* entertainments, but similar developments can be noted on the occasions when the monarch appeared in public and presented himself, as it were, to his subjects. The occasion was provided by the innumerable *entrées*, as they were called, of ruling princes into towns they had conquered or merely into places in their own dominions where they wished to display their magnificence and their might. The medieval and Renaissance monarchs were continually 'on progress,' and the chief towns they visited vied with one another to make the royal *entrée* as magnificent as possible. During the medieval period the emphasis was on the religious aspects of the kingly office. The king entered the town with his vassals in the full pomp of heraldry and proceeded with them to Mass in the cathedral. The celebrations near by always included a banquet and a tournament, and the tournament, modified into a harmless game, persisted for several centuries. But even the early *entrées* were not without certain theatrical elements. For the procession of Queen Isabella of Bavaria in Paris in 1389 a series of stages was contrived along the route, each with its symbolical tableau.

---

[1] Max von Boehn, *Modes and Manners*, translated by Joan Joshua (London, 1932–35), vol. i, pp. 297–298.

For the *entrée* of Charles VII in 1437 there was a mime of the Resurrection and a combat of the Seven Deadly Sins and the Seven Cardinal Virtues. Even the *entrée* of Charles VIII into Paris in 1482 was still strictly traditional; but by the early sixteenth century the pattern had been modified in conformity with the new ideas. The *entrée* of Anne of Brittany into Paris in 1504 was the last to contain a preponderance of religious motifs. When in 1507 her husband, Louis XII, entered Milan his victorious procession was preceded by the car of Mars. It only remained to identify the monarch himself with Caesar.

It has been suggested[1] that the transition from the old to the new was facilitated by the popularity of the legend of the Nine Worthies with its jumble of Joshua, David, Judas Maccabaeus, Hector, Caesar, Alexander, Arthur, Charlemagne, and Godfrey of Bouillon. Traces of this legend, with the list of Biblical, classical, and medieval heroes already complete, are to be found as early as the beginning of the fourteenth century. Gradually the classical element predominated, until only one hero remained, and he, of course, was Caesar. Henceforward the thread on which royal festivities were strung was the frank glorification of the monarch as hero.

The impulse, naturally, came from Italy. When, in 1548, Lyons offered to Henri II a pageant with all the participants dressed as ancient Romans it was essentially an undertaking of the Italian colony in that city, and the commemorative volume was published in the Italian language. Two years later he was received at Rouen in similar fashion, and his *entrée* into Orléans in 1551 was entirely *antiquisant*.

The Holy Roman Empire, with perhaps more justification than France, seized upon the idea of the 'triumph,' and identified first Maximilian and then Charles V with Caesar. The "Triumph of Maximilian" never actually took place, but it left a splendid record of its intended magnificence in a series of woodcuts, some of which were designed by Hans Burgkmair and the blocks for which are still in existence in Vienna. In the Albertina also is the splendid drawing by Dürer of the Emperor's triumphal car with its attendant nymphs. Many

[1] Joseph Chartrou, *Les Entrées solennelles et triomphales à la Renaissance (1484–1551)* (Paris, 1928).

of the figures in the procession are in medieval armour, but the classical element is also present, as well as a new hint of exoticism. For now Europe was beginning to awake to the fact that people in distant climes wore strange and characteristic costumes. The Turks were already making their presence felt, and it was known that they wore turbans. Europe was beginning to be conscious also of "Americans" with feathers in their hair, and the "wild men of the woods" dear to the medieval mind began to acquire "a local habitation and a name." For the Rouen *entrée* of 1550 the municipality constructed a Brazilian forest on the banks of the Seine and provided it with suitable inhabitants.

The figures of antiquity, however, still played the chief rôle in the imagination of the men of the sixteenth century, and they were brought on at every festivity. At the wedding of Cosimo de' Medici and Eleanor of Toledo, which took place in Florence in 1539, nymphs and sirens, tritons, fauns, satyrs, and shepherds sang and danced. When Francesco de' Medici married Joanna of Austria the bridal pair was attended by Venus and the Graces, Jupiter, Juno, Saturn, Mars, and Amor, together with figures representing Hope, Fear, Joy, and Pain carried over from the moralities of the Middle Ages.

Queen Maria of Hungary, Stadtholder of the Netherlands, offered such magnificent entertainments to her brother, the Emperor Charles V and her sister, Queen Eleanor of France, that they became proverbial. At one of these a castle was stormed by a thousand men, and defended by ladies dressed as nymphs—that is to say, in diaphanous draperies that displayed their legs and sometimes exposed their breasts. This Folies-Bergère element undoubtedly accounted for a good deal of the enthusiasm for such performances.

In France it was the same story. At the ball given in the Louvre to celebrate the marriage of the Dauphin with Mary Stuart there was a procession of galleys on wheels, figuring scenes from the life of Jason. When Margaret of Valois (later to be celebrated as "la Reine Margot") married the future King Henri IV a revolving stage was erected in the Palais Bourbon. On this twelve nymphs reclined. On the other side of the hall was Hell, peopled by demons. It is interesting to note that this survival from the mysteries was no longer contrasted with the Christian

Heaven but with a pagan Elysium. Knights tried to carry off the nymphs, who were defended by other knights. Cupid at last appeared and made peace, whereupon knights and nymphs danced together, and the festivity was concluded with a display of fireworks.

Sometimes such performances took place out of doors, and the one given on the occasion of a meeting between Charles IX and his sister, the Queen of Spain, has been described in her memoirs by Margaret of Valois, who was present. The scene was an island off Bayonne, and the mistress of ceremonies the redoubtable Catherine de' Medici:

> Nature seemed to have made ready the ballroom with her own hand, for there, right in the heart of the island, stood a great oval meadow girt with giant trees, in the shadow of which the Queen-Mother had great niches placed all around and in each niche a table laid for twelve. On four grass steps at one end of the space rose the royal board. The tables were served by detachments of shepherds and shepherdesses, clad in satin and cloth-of-gold in the costumes of the various French provinces. The crossing from Bayonne to the island was accomplished in richly decorated gondolas and canoes, around which sported tritons and sea-gods blowing horns and warbling sweet songs. On either side of the landing-place the shepherds and shepherdesses footed the appropriate dances of their province. . . . After this entertainment, and when the tables had been cleared, satyrs bore in a brightly lighted rock; upon this rock perched nymphs whose beauty and magnificent jewels radiated an even greater brilliance than the artificial lights illuminating the rock. Then the nymphs climbed down and danced a ballet, the perfect beauty of which so angered envious fortune that a violent storm arose with thunder and rain. The confusion in getting back by boat that night caused as much fun next morning as had the festivity itself.[1]

Royal and ducal personages loved to play an active part in such performances. At a fashionable wedding in Germany the Archduke Ferdinand of Austria appeared as Jupiter and the Duke of Brunswick as Apollo. Sometimes the fête ended badly. At a masquerade held at Waldenburg Castle in 1570 the tow garments of Count Georg and Count Eberhard von Hohenlohe, who were disguised as wild men of the woods, caught fire from a torch, and both were burned to death. Such wild men constantly figured in pageants, and it is interesting to note that as early as the reign of King Charles VI of France, in 1393,

[1] Quoted by Max von Boehn, *Modes and Manners*, vol. ii, p. 249.

similar costumes—of close-fitting linen garments covered with glue and stuck with loose flax—were responsible for similar deaths. This was the famous "Bal des Ardents" in which four great nobles lost their lives, the King himself only escaping by chance.

Festivities in England were, no doubt, on a smaller scale than those we have been describing, but the mythological element was seldom lacking in the entertainments offered to Queen Elizabeth. The most notable was that given by the Earl of Leicester at Kenilworth in 1575. Unfortunately, there is no pictorial record of this or similar English fêtes. It is not until we come to the following reign that we find a series of plates engraved by William Kip after Stephen Harrison showing the triumphal arches erected in 1603 for the entrance of James I into London. What would we not give for engravings of the costumes, especially as we know that Shakespeare marched in the procession.

The fêtes of the Netherlands are better documented. For the *entrée* of the Archduke Ernest into Antwerp in 1594 we have elaborate illustrations, one of which shows a large amphitheatre peopled with rows of women in pseudo-classical costume and six men dressed as Roman warriors. In commemoration of the triumphal progress through the Low Countries of Albert and Isabella we have two elaborate volumes.[1] It is interesting to note that in both the titles the ancient Roman device S.P.Q.R. has been transformed into S.P.Q.A.—i.e., *Senatus Populusque Antwerpiensi*. There was in the procession a triumphal car of Neptune and Hercules with eighteen girls as nymphs. One triumphal car represented an elephant, with *angels* singing in the howdah—an amusing combination of medieval elements with the new exoticism.

This curious blend of old and new is, as we have already noted, seen to best advantage in the pictures (now in the Victoria and Albert Museum) painted by Denys van Alsloot of the fête in Brussels in 1615. This was essentially a procession of moving stages. Those representing

---

[1] *Historica Narratio Profectionis et Inaugurationis Serenissimorum Belgii Principum Alberti et Isabellae Austrae Archiducum. . . . Auctore Ioanne Bochio S.P.Q.A. A Secretis. Antwerpiae, Ex Officina Plantiniana apud Ioannem Moretum. CIƆ. IƆCII.*

Pompae Triumphalis et Spectaculorum in adventu et inauguratione Serenissimorum Principum Alberti et Isabellae, Austrae Archiducum, Burgundiae ac Brabant. Ducum, S.R. Imperij Marchionum, in eiusdem Principatus metropoli, Antwerpia exhibitorum, graphica desiquatio; a Ioanne Bochio S.P.Q. Antwerpiensi a secretis scriptis illustrata. CIƆ.IƆCII.

Biblical scenes have been described in the previous chapter; in the present connexion the two most important were the car of Apollo and the car of Diana. Diana and her nymphs are clad in white flowing garments adapted from the female dress of the day—they wear ruffs. Apollo's Muses are more variously garbed in dresses and cloaks of different colours.

It was in Italy, however, that the most important developments took place. At Florence, especially at the enlightened Court of the Duke of Tuscany, no opportunity was lost of presenting magnificent triumphs, with a wealth of allegorical cars and mythological *intermezzi*. It is in these that we find the germ of opera and ballet.

In 1585 Francesco, Grand Duke of Tuscany, for the marriage of his sister to Cesare d'Este, arranged an elaborate series of festivities, of which we have a record,[1] unfortunately without pictures. There are, however, elaborate descriptions of the scenery and costumes, from which we learn that Beauty was represented by "a most beautiful girl, with blonde hair like gold-thread, her breasts exposed but modestly and with grace." The costume of Venus, however, was "*lascivissimo*, as befitted the Mother of Love." An *amorino*, like Adam and Eve in the mysteries, was clothed in a skin-tight garment of leather which made him appear nude.

This fête was followed, in 1589, by an even more remarkable and influential series of performances. The festivities in honour of the marriage of Ferdinand I of Tuscany to Christina of Lorraine included, in addition to the usual processions, hunts, mock tournaments, and banquets, three comedies, all enlivened with *entr'actes*, or interludes, providing a number of spectacular pantomimes *sul gusto antico*, interspersed with madrigals. The inventor of the *intermezzi* of 1589 was Giovanni de' Bardi, a pioneer of the *Riforma Melodrammatica* which was taking shape in Italy at the end of the sixteenth century. With him was associated Bernardo Buontalenti, as machinist and designer of the costumes.

---

[1] Bastiano de' Rossi, *Descrizione del Magnificentiss. Apparato e de maravigliosi Intermedi fatti per la Commedia Rappresentata in Firenze nello felicissime Nozze degl' Illustrissimi, ed Eccellentissimi Signori Il Signor Don Cesare d'Este, e la Signora Donna Virginia Medici* (in Firenze, mdlxxxv).

Design for ballet costume by Jean Bérain
late seventeenth century

For the history of stage décor the *intermezzi* of 1589 are of the utmost importance, but this is outside the scope of the present volume. Fortunately, there is in the Victoria and Albert Museum, in addition to four bistre drawings of the scenes, a coloured drawing of two female figures in costume, and these give a very clear notion of the kind of pseudo-classical costumes favoured at this period.

The most important of Buontalenti's pupils was Giulio Parigi, son of Alfonso Parigi who had assisted Vasari in his work at Florence. Giulio was responsible for the Grand Ducal fêtes of 1606, 1608, 1615, and 1616, and a good deal of evidence for these has survived, for they were etched by R. Cantagallina, Stefano della Bella, and Jacques Callot. An engraving by the last-named is one of the most valuable documents of the period that have come down to us. It shows the performance of an *intermezzo* in what is presumably the great hall of the Uffizi. A group of dancers in Roman costume, with towering plumes on their helmets, is descending from the stage by two ramps leading to the floor of the hall. Here they perform in an oval space left by the spectators.

The influence of the Florentines soon spread over Europe. We know, for instance, that Inigo Jones visited Italy between 1596 and 1604 and spent a considerable portion of his time in Florence. He returned home full of enthusiasm for the Italian innovations, and, as he was, from 1605 to 1640, responsible for the masques and other entertainments at the English Court, it was through him that the Italian influence made itself felt in England. Fortunately there is ample documentation, for not only do we have descriptions of the English Court masques by Ben Jonson, but a very considerable number of drawings by Inigo Jones himself, preserved in the collections at Chatsworth.[1] The earliest for which we have any data was entitled *The Queene's Masque of Blacknesse*; it was written by Ben Jonson and performed on January 6, 1605. For this and for *Hymenaei*, performed exactly a year later, only costume designs have survived. In addition to drawings of scenery there are many designs for the costumes in later masques. As might be expected,

---

[1] See *Designs by Inigo Jones for Masques and Plays at Court*, with introduction and notes by Percy Simpson and C. F. Bell (Walpole Society, vol. xii, Oxford, 1924). See also Enid Welsford, "Italian Influence on the English Court Masque" (*Modern Language Review*, October 1923).

most of these follow, with modifications, the costumes of antiquity, the men wearing a modification of the Roman tunic and the women the dress of their own time, suitably fantasticated, and with a remarkable degree of décolletage. Some of the dresses, especially those worn by the Court ladies, were extremely rich and must have cost their wearers considerable sums of money. The costumes of those who took part in the humorous interludes gave more scope for fancy, and here we find Inigo making use of Elizabethan and even of medieval costumes, as well as of animal disguises. In one of the antimasques there is an "Indian man" with a bow slung at his back and a crown of upstanding plumes. Another design is for "a Pagode," a figure with a pagoda-like head-dress and elongated fingernails. This, although described as worshipped by "Indians," must be one of the first examples of pseudo-Chinese costume in theatrical history. Some of the antimasques gave an oppor-tunity to introduce the costumes of the lower classes: "Porter," "Vintner's Boy," and "Kitchenmaid." Merlin in *Britannia Triumphans*, performed in 1638, wears a slashed and beplumed turban. We find also a "Persian," an "Arab," and a "Dwarf in Dress." *The Queene of Aragon* is the last masque of which we have any record. The troubles of the Civil War put an end to courtly entertainments.

In Germany the Thirty Years War had the same effect, but before its outbreak in 1618 there had been a perfect orgy of *entrées*: at Heidelberg, to celebrate the reception of the Order of the Garter by Frederick of the Palatinate, husband of Elizabeth of England, daughter of James I; at Stuttgart, in honour of John Frederick of Württemberg; and at Tübingen, for the birth of a son to John Frederick of Branden-burg. This last may be taken as typical of the early-seventeenth-century Court fête. It lasted from July 12 to July 20, 1618. On the first day there was a preliminary parade of the participants; on the second the baptism; on the third a *Schau-essen*, or great banquet; on the fourth and fifth days a procession with jousting; on the sixth day a ballet and a banquet; on the seventh a tournament of the Four Elements; on the eighth a hunt; and on the ninth, Sunday, a church service.

The mock tournament had by this time stereotyped itself into a *course de têtes et de bagues,* the first exercise consisting of slicing off the head of a dummy figure at full gallop and the second of 'riding at the ring,' a kind of tent pegging. It was usual to have four sets of competitors, known as *quadrilles,* and these troupes represented the Four Elements or the Four Quarters of the World, the latter being the more popular as offering scope for exotic costumes. The learned Jesuit Menéstrier, who attempted to lay down the rules for such performances,[1] tells us that "in France the first use of *quadrilles* was, if I am not mistaken, the *Courses à la Barrière,* performed by King Henri IV, at the Hôtel de Bourbon, in the year 1605." There was in the following year a *Carrousel des quatre Eléments* in the courtyard of the Louvre.

Fortunately, pictorial records of such festivities have survived. The Victoria and Albert Museum possesses engravings of the splendid pageants organized at Württemberg in 1609 and 1616, and in the same museum there is an illuminated drawing on vellum of a triumphal car attended by nymphs, the work of Hans Jörg Hochenmauer, later Hof-Contrafecter to the Emperor Ferdinand II.

The devastation of Germany between 1618 and 1648 caused the lead to pass once more to France. There were notable fêtes in the reign of Louis XIII, but it was reserved for Louis XIV to fuse all the elements of the old *entrée* together into one magnificent spectacle that served the double purpose of amusing his courtiers and impressing the world with his glory. The famous "*Carrousel* of Louis XIV" was staged in Paris in 1662 in the *Place* that still bears its name, and was commemorated eight years later by a superb volume (*Courses de Testes et de Bagues*), which is, indeed, the high-water mark of all such publications. The King himself appeared, inevitably, as a Roman Emperor with attendant warriors, and the three other parts of the *quadrille* represented Turks, Persians, and Americans, over whom the "Romans" were destined to be victorious in the feats of skill that were to follow. Such *quadrilles* had considerable influence on the development of stage costume, serving to popularize the supposed garb of Americans, Turks, and Romans.

---

[1] Claude-François Menéstrier, S.J., *Traité des tournois, ioustes carousels, et autres spectacles publics* (Lyon, 1669).

The challenge of "le Roi Soleil" could hardly be ignored by the Emperor, and in 1667 a magnificent fête was mounted in Vienna, a *gran balleto al Cavallo* with festival carriages and elaborate decorations. But the engraved records are vastly inferior to those of the French *Carrousel*.

Another sovereign who sought to outshine Louis XIV was Augustus II of Saxony. Tournaments had been very popular at Dresden in the sixteenth century, but by the end of the seventeenth they had become stylized, as all over Europe, into *courses de testes et de bagues*. A whole succession of fêtes was staged by Augustus, culminating in the masquerade of 1709 in honour of the visit of the King of Denmark. The entertainment consisted of a contest between the Seven Planets and Nimrod, followed by an opera-ballet in which the Planets took part, a *course de bagues* (riding at the ring) for ladies, a *carrousel* of the Four Quarters of the World, and other festivities.

The mention of an opera-ballet is significant; and it is interesting to note that ten years later it was thought necessary to include French comedies alternating with Italian comedies and opera. The composite form of Court entertainment was now out of date. The subsidiary amusements with which the *entrée* had been decorated and expanded had overbalanced the whole structure; or, to use another metaphor, the beads had become too heavy for the thread. The thread, which was essentially the Royal Procession, broke. The beads fell apart. The two most important of these beads were opera and ballet, and it is they, existing in their own right, which must be discussed in a later chapter.

Pageant costume. Drawing by Leonardo da Vinci, c. 1506–7
Reproduced by gracious permission of H.M. the Queen

Costume designs by Francesco Primaticcio

Costume designs by Francesco Primaticcio

Costume designs for opera or ballet
Franco-Florentine, c. 1590

Two designs f
masquers' costum
by Inigo Jon

ABOVE *Designs for grotesque costumes*
by Inigo Jones
RIGHT *Costume designs for French court ballet*
by Daniel Rabel, 1626

Costume design by Stefano della Bella

Costume design by Stefano della Bella

Costume design by Stefano della Bella

CHAPTER FIVE

THE COMMEDIA DELL'ARTE

I N any account of theatrical costume the *commedia dell'arte*, or Italian improvised comedy, must take an important place. It is, however, impossible, in a work like the present, even to summarize the learned controversies that have raged concerning its sudden appearance in the sixteenth century, the manner of its presentation, and its stock types.[1]

That these stock types bear a close resemblance to those of the Atellan farces such as Pappus, Bucco, Maccus, and Dossenus seems hard to deny: what scholars argue about is the connecting thread. It is hard to believe that strolling players were familiar figures in Western Europe during the Dark Ages. The Roman mime, however, may have persisted in the Eastern Empire and to have spread thence to Turkey, for there is a Turkish puppet drama that bears a resemblance to it. If the mimes persisted in Constantinople the fall of that city in 1453 may have driven actors as well as scholars westward, first to Cyprus, then to Venice and Rome. The *commedia dell'arte* may have been their rebirth in the West.

Certainly Duchartre[2] gives an impressive list of similarities that can hardly be accidental. Two of the characters in the Italian Comedy—

[1] For a full discussion of all the points involved see Allardyce Nicoll, *Masks, Mimes, and Miracles*.

[2] Pierre-Louis Duchartre, *La Comédie Italienne* (Paris, 1924). An English translation, *The Italian Comedy*, by R. T. Weaver, was published in 1929 by Harrap.

Arlecchino and Brighella—are called *zanni* (Shakespeare's "zanies"), a name that seems to be derived from the *sannio* of the Atellan farces, in spite of the fact that, as some scholars have argued, 'Zan' is merely the Venetian dialect word for 'John.' As Professor Nicoll points out, this connexion "may be illustrated still further by the fact that when other countries, inspired by Italy, came to name their clowns they also called them 'John'—Jean Potage, Hans Wurst, and Quanoushka-Douratchok." But the same authority finally comes down on the side of the *sannio* theory.

There were two kinds of *zanni*, one sly and one stupid. The stupid one is shown in an early print of the Italian Comedy with a bearded mask, and an actual mask of this kind, made of thick leather, has been preserved in the Musée de l'Opéra, in Paris. On the forehead is an enormous wart. Now, in the terra-cotta figurines of characters in the Atellan farces, Manducus is shown with a similar wart; and Nicoll concludes that it seems "probable that this stupid Zanni is a direct descendant, with a lineage through medieval secular drama, of the classic *sannio*, the *stupidus*, who, in his turn, was connected with the Atellan figures and with the bald-headed mime of Greece." It is known that the ancient mimes had shaven heads; the false scalps or headbands of the Italian comedians give the same effect. The slapstick (Shakespeare's "dagger of lath") and the phallus are common to both; so are the short garments worn by both the Italian valets and the ancient slaves. The quaint figure of Pulcinella (our Punch), with his crooked back and hooked nose, is to be found already in the Atellan Maccus. The Italian comedians, alone among their contemporaries, wore the mask, as did their ancient counterparts.

Whatever their origin, when we pick up the thread of these strange figures in the early sixteenth century we find that each character is firmly rooted in Italian soil, each, strangely enough, from a different Italian province and speaking a different dialect. Not only did they represent a cross-section of human life, they also formed a kind of geographical survey of the Italian peninsula. Arlecchino and Brighella hailed from Bergamo; Pulcinella was the sly Neapolitan; the pedantic Dottore came from the University of Bologna. Pantaloon was a

'Merchant of Venice,' and the loose trousers that he wore in the six-teenth century, and that are now universal, are called 'pantaloons' because of him.

Even more characteristic of him (for he did not always wear panta-loons) were his short jacket, usually of bright red, and his black, long-sleeved cloak. On his feet were soft Turkish slippers, and on his head he wore a little Greek cap. He had a grey moustache and a long white beard. His dark brown mask showed a hooked nose and some-times round spectacles. "He is the old father, the greedy merchant, the doting husband, the silly guardian, the aged counsellor."[1] Like his counterpart in Shakespeare, he is perpetually bewailing the treachery of his daughter and the loss of his ducats.

Other regions of Italy in turn produced their characteristic types— Milan, Beltrame and Scopin; Naples, first Pulcinella and then Scara-mouche and Tartaglia; Rome, Meo-Patacca, Marco-Pepe, and later Cassandrino; Turin, Gianduja; and Calabria, Coviello.

We must try to pick our way amid this multiplicity of types. The most famous of all is, of course, Arlecchino, who has come down to us as Harlequin. Yet when we first meet him his dress is very different from the stylish costume it eventually became. The earliest engravings show him merely as "a thing of shreds and patches," and it was not until early in the seventeenth century that the stylizing of the patches began. They became triangles of red, blue, and green arranged in a symmetrical pattern and separated by a narrow yellow braid. The triangles had become diamonds a hundred years later, and the soft cap adorned with a fox's brush or a hare's ears was exchanged for a pointed hat. From the first he carried a wooden sword and wore a black mask.

Brighella's mask, on the other hand, is of a sinister olive-green. Like Arlecchino, he is a valet with few scruples—in fact, even fewer, for he does not hesitate to use the knife. Nicoll describes him as "cruel, libidinous, cynically witty and self-seeking"; but, owing to the fact that he often appears under other names (he is Buffetto in an engraving by Jacques Callot), it is difficult to be sure of his identity before the

[1] Nicoll, *op. cit.*

seventeenth century. His characteristic dress was at first a loose-fitting white tunic and pantaloons, but this costume is distinguished from that of other *commedia dell'arte* figures by a series of horizontal stripes of green braid across the front of the coat. Transferred to the waistcoat, these horizontal stripes have persisted to our own day in the dress of liveried servants. Brighella had a large progeny in both Italy and France. One might say that Scapin and Sganarelle are his sons and Figaro his grandson.

An even more familiar figure was Il Dottore, whose speech was in the dialect of Bologna interlarded with Latin words and phrases to parade his learning. He was usually a lawyer (the University of Bologna was the centre of legal studies), occasionally a medical man—but rarely so before the late seventeenth century. He wore black clothes with a white collar and the academic cap and gown. The clothes worn underneath the gown followed contemporary fashion, and in the seventeenth century the small black toque was exchanged for a large black felt hat, but the gown remained unchanged, for he was always the doctor and the don, the caricature of an eternal type, the revenge of the ordinary man against learned pretensions.

The mask is very curious, covering only the forehead and the nose. Goldoni tells us that it "took its form from a birthmark which disfigured the face of a Paris consult of those days." The cheeks were rouged, and for the greater part of his history Il Dottore wore a small pointed beard.

Il Capitano was another important member of the *commedia dell'arte*—indeed, he is one of the earliest types known to us. "No one," says Professor Nicoll, in the valuable work from which we have already quoted, "knows exactly how this type arose. Some would make him a descendant of a type in the ancient mime. . . . Others see in him only an imitation of the Plautan *miles gloriosus*. Still others regard him as born independently in the Renascence of the contempt and hatred felt by Italians toward their Spanish tyrants." For Il Capitano was nearly always a Spaniard, and he followed the military fashions of his day, preserving, however—as the Spaniards themselves did—the modes of the sixteenth century well into the seventeenth. At first he wore a flesh-coloured mask with a big nose and fierce moustache, but the later Captains discarded this and simply powdered the face.

We have already mentioned the crooked back and hooked nose of Pulcinella. He is, perhaps, the most puzzling as well as the most fascinating of the stock types of the Italian Comedy. Like Arlecchino and Brighella, he is a servant, and his character is a mixture of folly and shrewdness, with a dash of villainy. There has been much controversy concerning the origin of his name, and whether or no he can be traced back to ancient times. In spite of the scepticism of some scholars it would seem that, as he has the same hooked nose and prominent chin, the same protruding belly and humped back, as some of the terra-cotta figures that have come down to us from the days of the Atellan farces, these resemblances cannot be accidental.

In the Italian Comedy he is a Neapolitan, and originally seems to have worn a version of the local costume of the peasants of the surrounding district. A loose blouse of white linen, caught in at the waist with a wide belt, and wide pantaloons were the essentials of his outfit. An engraving by Callot shows him, in the early seventeenth century, wearing these loose clothes together with a pointed hat, moustaches, and a beard. Later in the seventeenth century cock-feathers were added to the hat. The exaggeration of the hump, the shortening of the pantaloons, and the addition of striped stockings give us the Punch we know to-day, for, shrunk to a puppet, he is the most persistent of the Italian Comedy types.

Unless, of course, we consider that Pierrot has not only outlasted him but has kept his human stature and has even multiplied himself into a 'troupe of pierrots'—which, from the point of view of the *commedia dell'arte*, is an absurdity, for the original was essentially *one* character. Originally he seems to have been a variant of Pulcinella, but nothing is known of the costume he wore in the sixteenth century—if, indeed, he can be traced back so far. By the late seventeenth century he had assumed the costume that is still familiar to us—the loose white clothes with large buttons (which afterwards became pompons), the wide frilly ruff, the white skullcap with the white conical hat worn over it. He wore no mask, but his face was powdered white. He was a valet, like

Arlecchino and Pulcinella, but more personable, more sentimental, more naïve. He was much given to melancholy and was capable of love.

We must now turn to the 'serious' characters in the Italian Comedy, or, as we would say, the 'straight' parts. The typical scenario (which was often diverged from) required, in addition to 'the masks'—*i.e.*, two old men (Pantaloon and Il Dottore), two *zanni* (Arlecchino and Brighella), and a Capitano—certain characters who appeared without masks. These were, in general, two male lovers, two female lovers (*innamorate*), and a servant-girl. The last had various names, of which the most interesting is Columbina. The lovers wore the fashionable costume of their own day, and although the women did sometimes wear a mask it was only a little black velvet *loup* just covering the eyes. This ceases to have any theatrical significance when we realize that in the seventeenth century it was worn by the ladies in the audience as well. The servant began by dressing as a peasant girl, until, at the very end of the seventeenth century, she turns into Harlequina, whose costume is a mere echo of Harlequin's, as Pierrette's is of Pierrot's. The Columbine of modern pantomimes is badly 'out of period,' for her dress is merely the traditional *tutu* of the ballet dancer, which began to assume its final shape about 1830.

The most famous *innamorata* was Isabella Andreini, who belonged to the troupe of the Gelosi. Henri III of France saw their performance in Venice, on his way back from being King of Poland, and invited them to come to Blois in 1577 for the opening of the States-General. Another company, that of Ganassa, had already been seen in France, for they came to Paris in 1571 for the marriage festivities of the young King Charles IX, and so great was the enthusiasm they aroused that royal personages mingled with the comedians (probably playing the lovers' parts), as can be seen in a painting by Porbus now in the Museum at Bayeux. This created a scandal, and it was only the protection of the King that prevented the Italian players being expelled from France. Henri III treated the Gelosi troupe with still more indulgence, even allowing it to charge for admission. It was when their leader Andreini returned to Florence in 1578 that he married the sixteen-year-old Isabella. She was an outstanding success both for her beauty and for her acting ability, and she and her companions were received with enthusiasm in all the Courts of Northern Italy. They made another visit to France in 1588, but were frightened away by a decree of the Parlement against them. Henri IV, however, had sufficiently pleasant memories of them to summon them once more to Paris for his marriage with Marie de' Medici. We know that they were acting at Fontaine-bleau in November 1602 and were permitted to give public performances in the Hôtel de Bourgogne.

Louis XIII was equally fond of the Italian Comedy, and some of the troupes remained for several years in the French capital. The famous Scaramuccia, Tiberio Fiorelli, was especially popular, and is said to have soothed the two-year-old Dauphin (the future Louis XIV) by his grimaces. We know that Molière had the greatest admiration for him. Louis XIV, when he grew up, favoured the comedians, and there was a permanent company in Paris from 1662 until the unfortunate day in 1697 when they offended Mme de Maintenon by putting on a play called *La Fausse Prude*. They were peremptorily banished, and their theatre was shut up and sealed by the police.

Even their memory, however, was not without its effect, particularly on French painting. Watteau, indeed, is unthinkable without them, in spite of the fact that he himself never saw an actual performance of the *commedia dell'arte*. When he arrived in Paris it had been banished, but in the studio of his master Claude Gillot he found a large number of drawings and sketches showing the attitudes and costumes of the principal characters in the plays at the Hôtel de Bourgogne. Watteau fell completely under their spell, but for him the characters in the Italian Comedy were creatures of the imagination. Investing them with his own poetic vision, he transported them into a dream world of elegant melancholy, a world in which Harlequin and Brighella shed their grossness, their extravagant gesticulations, their Italian *brio*, a world in which Pierrot and Columbine flirted by moonlight, per-petually about to embark for a Cythère they were destined never to reach.

This world of Watteau was a real creation, a new country of the imagination exploited since by artists as diverse as Verlaine and

Picasso. Certainly Watteau inhabited it for the rest of his short life. The Comte de Caylus tells us that he had a collection of *habits galants et comiques* in which he loved to clothe his models. But he posed his models in natural attitudes, and was careful not to give them the exaggerated gestures of the theatre. The very poetry and naturalness with which Watteau invests his figures make his works less valuable than those of Gillot as documentary evidence of actual performances.

In England the records are much more meagre. It is possible that the well-known Arlecchino, Giovanni Alberto Ganassa, who was in Paris in 1571 and 1572, may have visited London. Prevented by an *arrêt* of Parlement from giving public performances in France, a company of Italian comedians did come to London at that time, for the performance was described by the Earl of Lincoln as "an Italian playe, and dyvers vautors and leapers of dyvers sortes verie excellent." In the autumn of 1573 we hear of a performance at Nottingham, and in July of the following year an Italian troupe accompanied Queen Elizabeth on her progress to Windsor and Reading. We know that it played in London, for "the unchaste, shameless and unnatural tomblinge of the Italian weomen" was attacked by a Puritan preacher.

We know that early in 1578 "one Drousiano, an Italian, a commediante, and his companye" were recommended to the Lord Mayor of London by the Privy Council, and therefore, presumably, given permission to perform. Drousiano Martinelli was one of the most celebrated Italian actors of his day, usually playing Arlecchino, and it is thought that he revisited England, with his wife Angelica, towards the end of the century.

That Shakespeare had seen performances of the *commedia dell'arte* seems certain. There is the famous reference to "the lean and slippered Pantaloon," and what is Justice Shallow but just such a character? Even Shylock, magnified as he is by the genius of the poet, is in essence but the miserly and deceived father of an *innamorata* in the Italian Comedy. Pistol is plainly a Capitano, swaggering and cowardly, and, indeed, some of the *double-entendres* given to him are curiously illuminated by a glance at Callot's etchings of the burlesque fencing matches of Scaramuccia and others.

Others besides Shakespeare were influenced, for of some of the comic characters in *Britannia Triumphans*, the masque performed at Whitehall in 1638, we find the following significant description:

> In the bottom row on the left is a Mountebanke's man or Zany. . . . Cap, with two feathers and long peak, drawn over his brow; loose blouse with hanging sleeves and baggy trousers. Next to him is a Harlequin. . . . He has beard and moustaches. Flat cap; long loose jacket, with sleeves covering hands; and trousers. Inscribed, '*harlekin*.' On the right is a Clown with moustaches and peaked beard. Close round cap or hood, loose jacket with large round buttons and belt, and trousers. Inscribed, 'John Farino.'[1]

Gian Farino was a well-known character in the Italian Comedy, and Harlequin and Zany need no comment. In another Whitehall masque, *Salmacida Spolia*, we find "a Doctor Tartaglia and a Pedant of Francolin." The latter is described as "a tall, thin man. . . . Long nose and pointed chin. Close cap with upturned brim. Tight-fitting doublet with large round buttons. Short trunk-hose, slashed and pulled, and tights. Long cloake falling to knees." What is this but the familiar Il Dottore?

During the Civil War and the Puritan domination that followed there was no place for the Italian comedians in England, but they returned soon after the Restoration. Tiberio Fiorelli is known to have been in London in 1673 and to have acted throughout the summer. In September King Charles II was pleased to bestow chains of gold and pieces of silver plate on "Scaramouchi and Harlekin." Two years later they returned and were permitted to use the Great Hall of Whitehall as a public theatre, "Scaramuccio acting daily . . . and all sorts of people flocking thither and paying their money as at a common playhouse," as Andrew Marvell tells us. John Evelyn, the diarist, saw one of their performances in September 1675. Fiorelli was in London again in 1678, and in the following year Giovan Antonio Lolli appeared as Il Dottore and Antonio Riccoboni as Pantaloon. But no English Gillot arose to depict their appearance and no English Watteau to be inspired by them. Harlequin, however, made a sufficient impression to become

---

[1] Walpole Society, vol. xii, p. 105.

the central character in English pantomime, although, strangely enough, he lost his voice in the process. Even as late as the present century a pantomime always concluded with a harlequinade, the last echo of a tradition that had had an immense effect on literature, art, and theatrical costume all over Europe.

Molière's costume as Sganarelle

Costume of Il Capitano in the Italian Comedy

Late eighteenth century

Costumes for Harlequin in the Italian Comedy

1695: Claude Gillot

Costumes for characters in the Italian Comedy

Pantaloon: late eighteenth century

Scaramouche: 1695: Claude Gillot

Italian Comedy scene. Hôtel de Bourgogne, Paris, c. 1630

CHAPTER SIX

COSTUME
IN SHAKESPEARE'S PLAYS

ACCURATE information concerning the clothes worn in the earliest production of Shakespeare's plays is sadly deficient. In J. de Witt's well-known drawing of the interior of the Swan Theatre in 1596 it is unfortunately impossible to distinguish the costumes of the characters: they are too sketchily drawn. Reference to a "doublet" in *Julius Caesar* has led scholars to suppose that, even in a play set in ancient Rome, the actors wore the dress of their own time. So, no doubt, most of them did, but there has survived *one* drawing, now in the possession of the Marquess of Bath, which shows seven characters in *Titus Andronicus* in 1595. The two soldiers in the drawing wear contemporary military dress, unless their breastplates and the plumed helmet of one of them might be supposed to be Roman. Two kneeling figures appear to be entirely Elizabethan, and Tamora wears a flowing robe —very different from the stiff contemporary farthingale—and a crown. But Alarbus wears a wreath on his head, a kind of breastplate, high boots or buskins, and a flowing cloak which probably conceals a short tunic. In a word, he is wearing an approximation to the costume *à la romaine* familiar to us in the pageants of the period. Aaron the Moor has a similar tunic and buskins, but not the turban that might have been expected. We find in this drawing the mixture of clothes of various styles and periods which audiences of the time took for granted. Other indications are almost non-existent except for a few literary references to "gorgious and sumptious" apparel. It is thought that the courtiers sometimes passed on their fine clothes to the actors.

One other early piece of evidence may be noted. There is a seventeenth-century engraving of the interior of the Red Bull Theatre at Clerkenwell. Several characters are shown on the stage—but not all from the same play. They have now been identified as the Changeling from the play of that name by Middleton and Rowley; a character from Robert Greene's *Tu Quoque; or, the Cittie Gallant*, a "French Dancing Mr"; Clause from *The Beggars' Bush*, by Beaumont and Fletcher; and, most important for our purposes, "Sr. I. Falstafe" and the "Hostes," from *Henry IV, Parts I and II*. The Hostess wears the ordinary clothes of a lower-middle-class woman in the Jacobean period. Falstaff is shown in doublet and breeches with turned-down, laced-topped boots, with a wide-brimmed hat and a falling collar edged with lace. It may have been the knowledge of this print that helped to stereotype the costume of Falstaff, for he is shown in very similar clothes throughout his career, even when his fellow-actors are wearing their own contemporary costume.

Professor Nicoll, with his extraordinary flair for discovering small items of what turns out to be important evidence, has unearthed[1] a sketch by Inigo Jones for a character in Sir William D'Avenant's *The Temple of Love*, produced in 1635. The sketch was inscribed by the artist: "a roabe of russet Girt low w^t a great belley . . . the sleeues shorte . . . buskines to shew a great swolen lege . . . a great head and balde." And Inigo adds, "like a Sr Jon fall staff." This is proof positive that the costume of Falstaff was already familiar as a definite type.

The 1709 *Shakespeare* edited by Nicholas Rowe poses some important problems, of which, for present purposes, the principal one is this: how far can the illustrations be used as representative of the actual costumes worn in contemporary productions of the plays? Moelwyn Merchant reminds us that "during this period many of the plays were never seen on the stage and any theatrical quality in the engraving must in those instances be due to the imagination of the engraver. On the other hand, *Coriolanus* is illustrated by a direct borrowing from a painting by Poussin,

[1] Allardyce Nicoll, *The Development of the Theatre*, pp. 180–181.

though, as it happens, the artist could have seen at least one version of
the play, Nahum Tate's rewriting of it as *The Ingratitude of a Common-
wealth.*"[1]

It would be out of place here to examine the plates in detail to decide
when the setting of the scene is "theatrical" and when it is picturesque.
It is the costumes only that concern us. "When the plates," says
Merchant, "are unambiguously influenced by stage practice there is a
mixed derivation from the contemporary theatre, from operatic and
masque conventions, and, when the play was rarely performed, from
conventions of a much earlier period." *Love's Labour's Lost* shows "the
plumes and the turbanned black attendant of an earlier courtly performance." The costumes in *A Midsummer Night's Dream* "have a suggestion of the operatic; Oberon's fairies are classically dressed, Titania's
are chastely contemporary." The characters in *Macbeth* wear the military uniforms of the early eighteenth century. Those in *Henry VIII* wear
early-eighteenth-century civil dress, except for the King, who is as
Holbein depicted him. In *Much Ado about Nothing* "Benedick and
Beatrice are in contemporary dress, Hero in the elaborate costume and
plumes of tragedy . . . the tonsured friar in a cotta goes very oddly with
his two ministers in gowns and bands, while Claudio is a figure frankly
of the previous age, in the Van Dyck convention which was the
eighteenth-century approximation to Tudor-Caroline dress."

In Quin's costume as Coriolanus (1749) there is certainly "a suggestion of the operatic," for, as can be seen from a contemporary engraving,
he played the part in a kind of ballet skirt. Breeches are seen below, and
buskins. The upper part of the costume consists of a kind of doublet
covered with embroidery and with double sleeves. On his head he
wears, over his full-bottomed wig, a helmet surmounted by the traditional plumes. Garrick abandoned this absurd costume in favour of
contemporary dress.

In early-eighteenth-century productions of *King Lear* all Lear's companions are as bewigged as the courtiers of Queen Anne. Lear himself
wears a plain version of their dress, but it seems to have been an
accepted convention that he should "wear his own hair"—that is, of

[1] W. Moelwyn Merchant, *Shakespeare and the Artist* (London, 1959), p. 48.

course, a wig representing his own white, flowing locks. He also wore a coat trimmed with ermine, this being the normal way of showing that a character was supposed to be a king. Richard III always wore one. So, presumably, did Macbeth, after his usurpation. Garrick "adopted the curious convention of having his ordinary eighteenth-century coat trimmed with ermine and of having a certain amount of loose hair attached at the back to a tightly curled, white-powdered, conventional wig."

Particular interest attaches to the costume of Macbeth. Did the Shakespearian stage present him as a Scotsman? Certainly not in anything that we should recognize as a kilt, if only because the kilt did not come into use in Scotland until the first quarter of the eighteenth century, and the belted-plaid for general wear was little more than a century older. Before that time what was worn was the *leine chroich*, or saffron linen shirt.[1]

If we may trust theatrical tradition it would seem that there was, originally and for long afterwards, no *special* costume for Macbeth. We know that Garrick played the part in the fashionable dress of his own day and actually in the King's livery. The credit of changing this has long been given to Macklin. Macklin produced the play at Covent Garden in 1773, when he was already an old man. He was already accepted as the Shylock of his age, but "Macbeth was sacred to Garrick." A lively controversy followed, but it is by no means clear what costume Macklin actually wore.

"For the ancient dresses (which will no doubt be copied at Drury Lane)," said the *Morning Chronicle*, "be it remembered that the first obligation is due to Mr Macklin"; and Thomas Davies, in his *Dramatic Miscellanies*, published in 1784, remarks that "The tragedy of Macbeth would still have been dressed in modern habits, if the good taste of Mr Macklin had not introduced the old highland military habit." But what *was* "the old highland military habit"?

In a contemporary line-engraving "sketched from life," he is shown

---

[1] For a learned and exhaustive discussion of this matter see "The Stage Costuming of Macbeth in the Eighteenth Century," by M. St Clare Byrne (*Studies in English Theatre History*, London, 1952).

wearing *breeches*. On the other hand a caricature, published in the same year, shows him wearing a kind of tunic, with a plaid, a Balmoral bonnet, and tartan stockings. The explanation of this apparent contradiction would seem to be that he wore both costumes, in different scenes of the play. Garrick himself had been toying for some time with the idea of using "the ancient dresses," and in January of the very year of Macklin's innovation he states in a letter, "I shall play Lear next week, and Macbeth (perhaps) in the old dresses with new scenes the week after."

Macbeth had been produced in Edinburgh in 1757, "new dress'd after the manner of the Antient Scots," and this probably inspired Macklin to imitation, but we must not imagine that anyone at this period had a very clear idea of what "ancient dresses" were like. Miss St Clare Byrne lends her great authority to the view "that from 1762 onwards an attempt was made, in the history plays only, to get away from contemporary dress." Public knowledge of historical costume was increasing. The antiquarian Strutt brought out his *Horda Angelcynnan* in 1776, and in the same year a dramatic critic complained that, in the revival of *Macbeth* at Covent Garden, Banquo "looked like a Saxon warrior, and Macbeth in his regal dress resembled the King of Diamonds." Did this mean that Macbeth wore a *tartan* tunic?

The whole problem is complicated by the existence of what was known as "the Spanish dress." This meant knee-breeches and a doublet, sometimes with puffed and slashed sleeves. It was established in the early eighteenth century, for Rowe, in 1709, shows Don John or Don Pedro wearing it in the bridal scene in *Much Ado about Nothing*. Miss Byrne says:

> Allowing for slight differences in the cut of the skirts of the doublet and for the substitution of heavy braiding or gold lace for the puffs-and-slashing ornament, the dress adopted for Scottish characters in the 1770's would appear ... to derive from the theatre's accepted Spanish dress. ... The general conclusion ... is that in London 'old' costumes of the Spanish type were adopted for *Macbeth* after Macklin's 1773 production, but that tartan was not necessarily used and that the tunic dress did not come into favour until adopted by Henderson and the Kemble brothers.[1]

[1] M. St Clare Byrne, *op. cit.*, p. 63.

Macklin is also credited with being the first to play Shylock in something other than contemporary costume. An engraving of him in the part carries the legend:

> This is the Jew
> That Shakespeare drew,

but 'drew' may have been used here in an imaginative sense. We do not know how Shakespeare dressed Shylock. In Macklin's innovation he wears a version of mid-seventeenth-century Dutch costume—*i.e.*, a long gown rather like a cassock, but with modifications which make it look like a long eighteenth-century coat, and falling bands. He wears his own hair (or a wig resembling real hair) loose about his shoulders, whereas Bassanio and the rest wear the tight, powdered, and curled wigs of the reign of George III.

Othello was dressed in the 'Turkish' costume which had long been a stage convention, with plumed turban, tunic, and sash. Another 'special' costume that was by now making its way was the Hungarian, with frogged tunic and fur cap. The employment of hussars in every European army had familiarized the public with this exotic dress. It was worn by characters such as Hippolyta in *A Midsummer Night's Dream*.

Hamlet, on the other hand, was played in ordinary dress, but usually of black and with one of his stockings down. Evidence of this is not lacking. A print of Henderson as Hamlet in 1776 shows him very elegantly attired with tie-wig, rabat, and lace ruffles. He might be the younger son of an English county family who has 'taken Holy Orders.' Indeed, *Hamlet* in modern dress was no invention of the twentieth century; it was the established custom of the eighteenth. Considerable interest, therefore, centres round a painting by Francis Hayman, the only survivor of four which he contributed to the decorations of Vauxhall Gardens. From contemporary descriptions we learn that

> on the west side of the Grove, to the right of the entrance to the Gardens, was a pavilion used by Frederick, Prince of Wales. There are put in four large paintings, done by the ingenious Mr Hayman, from the historical plays of Shakespeare . . . the storm in the play of *King Lear* . . . the representation of the play in the tragedy of *Hamlet* . . . a scene in *Henry the Fifth* . . . a scene in the *Tempest*.

It is the *Hamlet* painting that we have, and although "it is manifestly not chiefly a theatre study,"[1] Hayman was intimately connected with the theatre, for early in life he had been a scene-painter at Drury Lane, and it is probable that the position of the actors and the arrangement of the scenes are very like what they had been on the stage. It is even more probable that the costumes are the same, or similar, to those in an actual production (Garrick played Hamlet at Drury Lane almost every year during his career). Hamlet himself is not shown, but the King wears mid-eighteenth-century costume, and Gertrude also. Polonius wears his own hair, but is otherwise in clothes of the same period.

As late as 1794 we find Stephen Kemble (as depicted in a caricature by Robert Dighton) playing Hamlet in the dress of the seventeen-nineties. But eleven years before, when John Philip Kemble appeared as Hamlet at Covent Garden, he was already wearing a kind of pseudo-Elizabethan costume (except for the Van Dyck falling collar) with puffed sleeves and trunk-hose. This was the mode that prevailed for the next generation. Henry Johnson wore it in 1798, and so did Edmund Kean at Drury Lane in 1814.

But soon, with the dawn of the historical sense, people began to feel that Elizabethan costume—or some approximation to it—was unsatisfactory. Hamlet, surely, had lived at a much earlier period. There was that awkward reference in the text to the Danish invasions. So attempts began to be made to push the costume further back. The trunk-hose gave place to a kind of knee-length tunic supposed to be medieval but not very close to any historical costume that has ever existed. By the middle of the century this tunic, with the occasional addition of a seventeenth-century lace collar, had become the accepted mode. Samuel Phelps wore it at Sadler's Wells in 1847, Macready at the Haymarket Theatre in 1849, Barry Sullivan in 1852, Charles Kean at the Princess's Theatre in 1850. But Edwin Booth in 1880 wore a costume that plainly tried to get back to the actual period of the Danish invasions: rough tunic, cross-gartering, etc.

---

[1] W. Moelwyn Merchant, *Shakespeare and the Artist*, p. 46. See also Laurence Gowing, "Hogarth, Hayman and the Vauxhall Decorations" (*Burlington Magazine*, vol. xcv, No. 598, January 1953, pp. 4–19).

The thirst for historical accuracy (whatever, in the case of many of Shakespeare's plays, that could possibly mean) had been growing ever since the eighteen-twenties, and was due, very largely, to the influence of Planché. J. R. Planché was not only a librettist, an authority on heraldry, and Rouge Croix Pursuivant, but a designer for the stage and the author of a *History of British Costume*. In him the antiquary and the costume-designer met, and he was therefore not likely to accept the approximations to historical accuracy that had formerly passed muster. He designed the costumes for *King John*, and the playbill issued shows his approach to the problem:

> This present Monday, January 19, 1824, will be revived Shakespeare's Tragedy of King John with an attention to Costume never equalled on the English Stage. Every Character will appear in the precise HABIT OF THE PERIOD, the whole of the Dresses and Decorations being executed from indisputable Authorities. . . . King John's Effigy in Worcester Cathedral . . . Queen Elinor's Effigy in the Abbey of Fontevraud. Effigy of the Earl of Salisbury in Salisbury Cathedral. . . . Illuminated Mss in the British Museum, Bodleian, and Bennet College Libraries . . . &c.

As Professor Nicoll says, "Planché put on what was undoubtedly the first completely 'historical' production of Shakespeare's drama, for he paid attention not only to the hero's costume but to those of the meanest underlings."[1] Previously, whatever the principal characters might have worn, the rest were clad simply in whatever was available in the theatrical wardrobe.

Planché's success—for "receipts for 400 to 600 pounds nightly soon reimbursed the management for the expense of the production"—encouraged emulation, and every effort was made to provide 'correct' costumes. Charles Kean, although by no means so great an actor as his father Edmund Kean, was an enterprising and educated man ("Charlie shall go to Eton," cried his father after his first major success), and he was determined to have an educative effect on the general public. For a series of splendidly mounted Shakespearian productions at the Princess's Theatre, London, in the eighteen-fifties he called in not only the best scenic artists of his day—Grieve, Telbin,

[1] Allardyce Nicoll, *The Development of the Theatre*, p. 191.

The Red Bull Theatre, Clerkenwell
c. 1672

Scene from Titus Andronicus
from a manuscript of 1595

Quin as Coriolanus, 1749

Macbeth and the Witches
from the first illustrated edition
of Shakespeare's Works, 1709

Costume for Comus, 1757

LEFT *Mr Smith as Alexan*
in The Rival Queens, *17*
BELOW *Mr and Mrs Barry as Jaff*
and Belvidera in Venice Preserv'
17

ABOVE *Mr Garrick and Miss Younge*
Tancred and Sigismunda, *1776*
BELOW RIGHT *Mr Yates as Malvolio*
Twelfth Night, *1776*

Mr Garrick as Macbeth, 1775

Mr Macklin as Shylock, 1775

Mr Webster as Douglas, 1778

Within the illustration:

J.Roberts del.   Publish'd for Bell's British Theatre Oct.r 6.th 1777.   Thornthwaite Sculp.t

Mrs Yates as Electra, 1777

Mrs Barry as Phaedra in Phaedra and Hippolitus, *1777*

Miss Younge as Cleopatra in
Antony and Cleopatra, *1776*

Mrs Bulkley as Mistress Ford in
The Merry Wives of Windsor, *1776*

Miss Brunton and Mr Holman as Palmira
and Zophna in Mahomet, *1786*

Edmund Kean as Richard III

David Garrick as Richard III: after Hogarth

ABOVE *Miss Stuart as*
Joan la Pucelle in
Henry VI, Part 1, *1786*
LEFT *Miss Brunton as*
Cordelia in King Lear
1785

RIGHT *Mrs Pope*
(formerly Miss Younge)
as Cleopatra, 1786
BELOW *Mrs Wells*
as Lavinia in
Titus Andronicus, *1785*

ABOVE *Mrs Barnes
as Anne Bullen
in* Henry VIII, *1786*
RIGHT *Mrs Kemble
as Juliet in*
Romeo and Juliet
c. *1780*

LEFT *Mrs Cuyler*
as Cressida in
Troilus and Cressida, *1785*
BELOW *Miss Farren*
as Olivia in
Twelfth Night, c. *1780*

Mr Wrench as Benedick in Much Ado About Nothing, *1814*

Miss Bolton as Ophelia in Hamlet, *1813*

Mrs W. West as Hermione in The Winter's Tale

Mrs Warner as Hermione, 1845

Mr Young as Hamlet, 1813

Miss Smith as Portia in
The Merchant of Venice, *1813*

Mr Wallack as Alessandro Massaroni
in The Brigand, *1830*

Mr Macready as Shylock

Mr Macready as Othello, 1826

Mr Macready as Macbeth

*Mr Macready as King John
and Mr Cooper as Hubert*

Mrs Fitzwilliam as Mistress Page in The Merry Wives of Windsor

Miss Glyn as Cleopatra

Miss Woolgar as Rosalind

Mr Charles Kean as Hamlet

Miss Vandenhoff as Juliet

Miss Glyn as Lady Macbeth

Miss Glyn and Mr Hoskins as Isabella and Lucio in Measure for Measure

Charlotte and Susan Cushman as Romeo and Juliet

Mr Phelps as Falstaff, 1846

Mr Edmund Kean as Othello

Salvini as Othello

Ira Aldridge as Othello, 1852

*Ada Rehan as
Rosalind in*
As You Like It

Lloyds, Gordon, Dayes—but learned men of all kinds, sometimes to the point of absurdity, as when he boasts, in his elaborate programme notes for *The Winter's Tale*, that the "vegetation peculiar to Bithynia is adopted from . . . drawings taken on the spot." But why *Bithynia*? Because in his thirst for realism Kean was unable to accept Shakespeare's "Sea-coast of Bohemia," and he "therefore followed the suggestion of Sir Thomas Hanmer, in his annotations of Shakespeare, by the substitution of *Bithynia*. The difference of name in no way affects the incidents or metre of the play, while it enables me to represent the costumes of the inhabitants of Asia Minor." Poor, ignorant Shakespeare. He had not only got his European geography all mixed up, but he had referred in the same play to "the Delphic oracle, Christian burial, an Emperor of Russia, and an Italian painter of the sixteenth century."

In the historical plays, however, we must certainly give credit to Charles Kean for striving to present them without the absurdities of previous productions. The Kean tradition has, on the whole, been maintained. But in the unhistorical plays (if they may so be called) the story has been very different. Their settings and costumes have varied from the extreme of 'realism' to every kind of theatrical, and even operatic, convention, until in 1925 Sir Barry Jackson set the fashion for 'Shakespeare in Modern Dress' by his production of *Hamlet* at the Kingsway Theatre, London. And so, at least so far as *Hamlet* was concerned, the wheel came full circle. We found ourselves back in the age of Garrick, or even in that of Shakespeare himself.

CHAPTER SEVEN

OPERA AND BALLET

IT is no easy matter to distinguish between the two *genres* of opera and ballet in the seventeenth century; nor is it easy to disentangle them from the Court fêtes that had given birth to both. Opera was saved from being a mere Court function by its popularity with the public. With its musical development we are not here concerned, but we may note that it spread from Florence all over Italy with astonishing speed, and soon established itself at Venice and Rome. Rome, indeed, was seized with a kind of madness for this new form of musical entertainment, and it was here, says Henri Prunières, that occurred the fusion of the spectacular *intermedii* of the princely Courts with Florentine lyrical tragedy. It was at Rome that the Borghese, and then the Barberini, achieved the transformation of musical tragedy into opera.

This transformation was essentially a matter of an added magnificence of décor and costumes. For their splendid new theatre in Rome, capable of holding 4000 spectators, the Barberini employed artists of the stature of Bernini to design the settings. Bernini did more than that, for John Evelyn tells us that for the Carnival of 1645 this universal genius painted the scenes, carved the ornamental statues, invented the machines, composed the music, and constructed the theatre! Presumably he also designed the costumes. All the aristocracy of Rome was engaged in these operations, and even the clergy became deeply involved. A Pope himself wrote operas. This was Clement IX, who as Monsignor Rospigliosi had been the official librettist of Pope Urban

VIII; and it is interesting to note that John Milton was present at a performance of his opera *Chi sofre, speri* in 1639. It was undoubtedly the décor of such pieces that excited most interest and left most records. We hear less of the costumes, but we know, for example, that Vitali's *Aretusa*, performed in 1620 in the presence of Cardinal Borghese, showed pastoral scenes in which nymphs and shepherds disported themselves. The costumes of the shepherds were of brilliant colours, and those of the nymphs were of silver gauze. Both costumes and décor were the work of Pompeo Caccini.

It was in 1637 at Venice that the first *public* representation of opera was given. Rome had a public opera-house in 1652, and Naples about the same time. The enthusiasm spread to Germany through the Courts of Munich and Vienna. Henrietta Adelaide of Savoy, wife of Duke Ferdinand, introduced it into Bavaria, and very soon it had spread northward to Hamburg, where a public theatre was built in 1678. In Vienna *Il Pomo d'Oro* was produced with décor and costumes by Burnacini, one of the greatest names in the history of theatrical costume.

In Paris Cardinal Mazarin erected in the Tuileries a superb theatre for the performance of Italian opera. It was inaugurated on the occasion of the marriage of Louis XIV to the Spanish Infanta in 1660; but long before this both opera and ballet (although it is impossible at this period to distinguish between them, so far as décor and costume are concerned) had been well known at the French Court. Designs by Daniel Rabel have survived for the royal ballets of 1626. Rabel in general followed the line of contemporary costume or that of the period just previous to his own. The masked female dancers in one of the designs preserved in the Louvre are clothed partly in the costume of the late sixteenth century, with puffed and slashed sleeves and farthingale, partly in the farthingale without the skirt. Except for the breeches with bows at the knees, which are thus made visible, this costume is a curious anticipation of nineteenth-century ballet dress. Such costumes were no doubt designed for a humorous ballet. For more serious works the Roman mode predominated. Heroes of all kinds wore, and were to wear for long afterwards, a version of Roman costume—or, rather, the Roman military tunic, which had now assumed a form which Caesar himself would not have recognized. The short tunic skirt was there, and the corselet, reproducing the form of the body even to the shape of the breasts, with almost always an animal-head set in the middle. The helmet had now sprouted plumes of a number and magnificence which the Romans never knew. This extravagant plumage of pseudo-Roman warriors goes back at least as far as the Florentine fêtes of the early years of the seventeenth century. We see them in some of the designs by Stefano della Bella, and we know that this artist was called to France in 1645 to provide the designs for *Finta Pazza*. Nine years later, for the famous *Noces de Thétis et de Pèle*, put on by Cardinal Mazarin at the Petit Bourbon, the Italian Torelli provided the scenery and the machines, and perhaps had a hand in the costumes. It is thought that some of them, however, were designed by Henri Gissey, *dessinateur du Cabinet du Roi*, who is said to have designed all the costumes for the splendid *Carrousel* of 1662. This is enough to remind us that a mock tournament and an opera were still thought of as part of the same entertainment.

Gissey having died, he was succeeded as *dessinateur du Cabinet du Roi*, in 1673 or early in 1674, by Jean Bérain. He was responsible in 1680 for the costumes for *Le Triomphe de l'Amour*, by Lully. This opera is notable as being the first occasion on which women appeared on the operatic stage. Some of the costumes designed for them by Bérain have more than a slight flavour of the Folies-Bergère, but we should remind ourselves that the body was not actually exposed but covered with a pink *maillot*. Furies and other unattractive females were still played by men.

There is a certain element of the exotic in Bérain's characters. He introduces Indians and Americans, as well as the inevitable Turks. He even has a Chinaman or two, but there is no attempt whatever at regional or historical accuracy. Nothing is more interesting, when studying the costume designs of Bérain, than to note how often, even when he is devising the costumes of legendary characters, his line is brought back to the dress of his own day.

This is still more noticeable in his female costumes, which, however fantastic they try to be, never quite lose the lines of contemporary dress.

It is here a laced corsage and there a suggestion of panniers. And, of course, the *applied decoration* is never anything but the purest Louis-Quatorze: many of the motifs might have been copied from the decoration of a boule cabinet. Indeed, they have no need to be copied: they were devised by the same hand. As a decorative artist Bérain dominated French taste, and hence the taste of Europe at this period, when even theatrical costume had a period style which the archaeologists and historians have never quite recaptured with their careful reconstructions. And although Bérain was certainly not as learned in these matters as his successors, he was not ignorant. It was simply that he was trying to do something else. He was trying to exalt the style of his own day (in the creation of which he was all the time playing an important part) to the limit of fantasy.

When Jean Bérain the Elder died in 1711 the great days of French Court festivities were over for a time. The disasters of the closing years of the reign of Louis XIV and the sobering influence of Mme de Maintenon threw a shadow over the gaiety of Versailles. He was succeeded by his son, Jean Bérain the Younger, who followed so closely in his father's footsteps that it is impossible to distinguish the work of the two men by their style. He seems to have made a veritable cult of his father's memory, and he is thought to have been responsible for the immense documentation of it that has come down to us. There are examples of Bérain's work in the Bibliothèque Nationale, in the Musée de l'Opéra, in the Bibliothèque de Versailles, in the Victoria and Albert Museum in London, and elsewhere. There is very little English documentation of opera at this period. Designs by Thornhill have been preserved, but, while these show very clearly the scenery for *Arsinoe, Queen of Cyprus*, performed in London in 1705, they give very little indication of the costumes worn.

After the death of Louis XIV there was a reaction against the grandeur and formality of his Court. So long had the old King reigned that his immediate descendants were dead before him, and he was succeeded by his great-grandson, Louis XV, who was a mere child. A few years later, when the young King was eleven, he found, to his disgust, that he was expected to appear as a dancer in the Court ballets.

He did so for the first time in the *divertissement* given at the performance
of Thomas Corneille's *L'Inconnu* in February 1720. A score or so of
young nobles took part also with *danseuses* of the Opéra as partners, and
it is curious to note that at these entertainments some members of the
public were admitted *sur billets*. Some members of the Court were
shocked that the King should appear in the company of *filles d'opéra* in
what was in effect a public entertainment; but the reply was that
Louis XIV had done it, and why should not Louis XV do the same?

The young King's next appearance was at the end of 1721 when in
the Théâtre des Machines constructed for Louis XIV by Vigarani in
the Tuileries he took part in the *Ballet des Eléments*. Louis was a shy
boy of twelve, and it is thought that these early experiences gave him
a permanent distaste for the theatre; but the occasion was an important
one from our point of view because it proved to be the starting-point
for an entirely different style in theatrical decoration. The theme of the
entertainment seems to have been tedious enough. It concerned the
Four Elements emerging from Chaos, and there were four *entrées*, each
with its appropriate mythological tableau. Air was represented by Ixion
and Juno, Water by Orion and Neptune, Fire by the "Vestal Emilie"
(whoever she may have been), and Earth by Vertumnus and Pomona.
A very short Epilogue introduced the King as the Sun God accompanied by his Court of the Signs of the Zodiac, the Four Quarters of
the World, and all the previous characters. It was a brilliant spectacle,
the whole of the resources of the Opéra having been mobilized for the
occasion. The décors were designed by Perrault and painted by two
Academicians, Antoine Dieu and J.-B. Audry. The costumes were the
work of another Academician, Claude Gillot.

We have already met Gillot when dealing with the *commedia dell'arte*,
and know of his interest in all things theatrical. His costumes on this
occasion created so much of a sensation that two years later, in 1723,
they were engraved by F. Joullain, and, although unfortunately these
are not in colour, they give us a very good idea of the clothes worn.
Among the engravings are eight costumes of tritons, five of furies, four
of fauns; others represent naiads, Plutus, and other characters.

Although the general line of Gillot's costumes differs little from that

Design for ballet costume by Louis-René Boquet
mid-eighteenth century

of Bérain, we can already see the beginnings of eighteenth-century taste. He kept the long skirts of the dancers and even extended their width by means of panniers, in accordance with the contemporary mode, but, says Carlos Fischer, "He made all these costumes infinitely lighter and more gay by suppressing the ornaments with which they were covered; he reduced the size of the plumes, the wigs, and the sleeves; he did not abuse the use of allegorical symbols, and only included the *attributs* that were indispensable. He gave butterflies' wings to the Hours of the Day, and bats' wings to the Hours of the Night. His nereids he clad in scales and shells. Time and Plutus wore Oriental turbans." The whole effect was that of an escape from formality into fantasy: the same words might be used for the transition from the Baroque to the Rococo, a characteristic of this epoch. Gillot died soon after this triumph, but as records of his work we have not only the engravings by Joullain, but a sheet of paper in the Louvre showing four costumes in colour. As might be expected, the colouring is very discreet and tender in accordance with the new mode.

Giovanni Niccolo Servandoni, carrying on the tradition of the wandering Italian theatrical decorator, dominated the French theatre for some years. In style he harked back to Bérain, but in 1744 he was succeeded at the Académie de Musique by François Boucher. Ten years before, Boucher had designed a whole series of stage costumes, but as book illustrations, and not for the theatre; and after working for four years at theatrical design he abandoned it because he recognized that it was not his *genre*. His easel pictures were probably more profitable, and his practice as a portrait-painter and decorator of boudoirs less exasperating than working for the stage must inevitably be at any period. In any case, certain of Boucher's theatrical designs have survived, and it is enough to say of them that they are not unworthy of the master.

Strangely enough, we know much more of the work of his successor, J.-B. Martin, an artist as obscure as Boucher is illustrious, and who succeeded him in 1748 as *dessinateur des Habillements de l'Opéra*. He remained such for some eight years, until 1756 or 1757, and in 1763 published a series of engravings after his designs which gave an excellent notion of his style. His female characters borrowed the *toilettes* of the fashionable woman of his day, slightly modified by various *garnitures*—a Medea wearing enormous panniers garnished with cabbalistic signs, an Indian queen with coloured plumes in her hair, a dryad with a border of oak-leaves, a fury with serpents—but serpents *mignons et gentils*—*Une Furie de Salon*, as Carlos Fischer calls them. We find a Neptune covered with shells and a Hercules clad in furs, but the realism is very thin. Everything is quite obviously in the *style Louis XV*, completely Rococo. In the place of magnificence there is grace, instead of the noble attitude the elegant gesture; the heavy embroideries have yielded to gay ribbons. In one sense the clothes are much simpler: light, closely fitting vests replace the Roman corselets, the materials are more delicate, the colours more tender. On the other hand, the Roman skirts have swelled out to astonishing proportions, and all the women are in wide hoops.

Martin must have the credit (if credit it be) of introducing the French peasant on to the stage. But what a transformation in the process! His peasant boys and girls never kept pigs or milked cows in that attire! They are all silks and satins with ribbons everywhere: the type that has been preserved for us in the porcelain figures of the period. When, a generation later, Marie-Antoinette played at being the milk-maid it was this kind of milkmaid she no doubt had in mind.

In the work of Louis-René Boquet we can see the same tendency even more plainly. Boquet had been attached to the *Menus Plaisirs* (what might be called the *private* performances at Court) since 1751, but from 1758 he was employed officially at the Académie Royale de Musique, and his style dominated the whole of French costume design from the middle of the eighteenth century almost until the Revolution. He was at the height of his powers in the seventeen-sixties, and a prodigious number of his drawings from this period have come down to us. The style is the style of his time, but there is something so personal in his interpretation of it that it is hardly necessary for his drawings to be signed. They conjure up an artificial world of mythological figures, small, neat heads carefully powdered and adorned with roses, a deep square *décolletage* over a corsage ending almost in a point, so narrow is the waist. Below that spreads out the billowing skirt: a wide canvas

*Design for ballet costume for Louis XIV
by Henri Gissey*

Costume design for the Carrousel of 1662
by Henri Gissey

Design for ballet costume, c. 1670

Design for ballet costume, c. 1650

*Design for ballet costume
by Henri Gissey*, c. 1670

Three designs for ballet costumes
by Henri Gissey, c. 1670

Two designs for ballet costumes
by Henri Gissey, c. 1670

*Design for ballet costume
by Jean Bérain
late seventeenth century*

153

*Two designs for ballet costumes
late seventeenth century*

by Jean Bérain

*Attributed
Jean Bérai*

*Two costume designs for ballet by Jean Bérain
late seventeenth century*

*Four designs for ballet costumes by
Jean Bérain, late seventeenth century*

*Design for ballet costume
by Jean Bérain
late seventeenth century*

*Costume design by Claude Gillot
for the* Ballet des Eléments
early eighteenth century

*Design for ballet costume
by Jean Bérain
late seventeenth century*

*Costume design by Claude Gillot
for the* Ballet des Eléments
early eighteenth century

Design for costume
by Louis-René Boquet

The Fitzgiggo R
showing the stage
Covent Garden Theatre, 1

*Design for costume
by Louis-René Boquet*

*...ge setting and costumes by
...Vrede at the Schauburg, 1749*

French ballet costumes
c. *1780*

treated almost as a separate picture over which riot all the delicate ornaments of Rococo.

His male figures are in ballet skirts too, but much shorter ones, and the upper part of their bodies is enclosed in a smooth vest-like garment fitting the figure. Fortunately, we have a drawing by Boquet—for the costume of the dancer Vestris as Plaisir—annotated in his own hand with directions for the materials to be used: "Fond de satin blanc, draperie de mosaïque d'argent de coupe rose. Bouffets en mosaïque rose et argent. Fleurs artificielles. Bouquet de pierreries sur le corps." It is the very form and pressure of the time, an image at once absurd and enchanting.

From one point of view the costume of Boquet—even more than those of Bérain—were the ideal clothes for the presentation of opera, as it was understood in his period. That it could not continue indefinitely, however, is obvious, if only because the costumes of the Court and of society were themselves changing. Bérain's costumes, and Boquet's too, were fantastications of contemporary dress with such minor concessions to character and period as a Turkish turban here and a Roman tunic there. Their fundamental lines changed with the fluctuations of fashion in the outside world.

What brought all this to an end was the growing knowledge of the costumes of former epochs and distant countries. Even Boquet sometimes diverged from his stylization to show us a Pole, a Chinaman, or a Negress, but his was always an *exotisme très mitigé*. The splendid unity of the *style Louis XIV* and the *style Louis XV* had been to some extent preserved by the ignorance of the spectators as regards the costume of far away and long ago. They did not know enough to be critical. It is perhaps arguable that a real *style* is impossible when the spirit of history has emerged. Once the mould of the Rococo had been broken up, the way was clear for the pursuit of 'historical accuracy.' Most lovers of the theatre (and therefore of the theatrical) would to-day be inclined to regard the change from the stylization of Boquet to the fumbling attempts at realism that followed as a disaster, and would be tempted to echo Carlos Fischer's admirable phrase: "Nous verrons, hélas! que le costume d'opéra, étant désormais consacré à l'Histoire, n'a plus d'histoire!"

CHAPTER EIGHT

FROM NOVERRE TO DIAGHILEV

Two influences tended to modify, and finally to destroy, the conventions of Rococo opera and ballet. One, already mentioned, was the growing knowledge of historical and regional costume among educated people; the other was the increasing elaboration of dancing technique. As far as the first is concerned opera and ballet were equally affected; and even as regards the second they had now become so intimately linked, they had become so much part of the same entertainment, that they can be treated together.

The great innovator was the famous *maître de ballet* Jean-Georges Noverre, who published his *Lettres sur la Danse* in 1760. "Obstinacy in adhering to worn-out tradition," he said,

> is the same in every part of opera. . . . Greek, Roman, Shepherd, Hunter, Warrior, Faun, Forester, Games, Pleasures, Laughs, Tritons, Winds, Fires, Dreams, High Priests, Celebrants—all these characters are cut to the same pattern and differ only in the colour and ornaments with which a desire for ostentatious display rather than good taste has caused them all to be bespattered at caprice. Tinsel glitters everywhere; Peasant, Sailor, Hero—all are covered alike. The more a costume is decorated with gew-gaws, spangles, gauze and net, the greater the admiration it procures in the ignorant spectator.[1]

He proposed to do away with the *tonnelet* and the *paniers*, and to substitute

> light and simple draperies of contrasting colours worn in such a manner as to reveal the dancer's figure . . . beautiful folds, fine masses with the ends fluttering

[1] Jean-Georges Noverre, *Letters on Dancing and Ballets*, translated by C. W. Beaumont (London, 1930).

and producing ever-changing forms as the dance becomes more and more animated, everything should convey a sense of filminess.[1]

For some time both male and female dancers, but especially the women, had been increasingly impatient of the hampering clothes in which they were expected to perform. As early as 1730 Camargo, the first *danseuse* to attempt the *entrechat*, had shortened her skirt to mid-calf. "Camargo, moreover," says Cyril W. Beaumont,

> had the forethought to wear a small pair of close-fitting knickers while executing her new *temps d'élévation*, a tremendous innovation if it be recalled that knickers did not come into general wear, at any rate in England, until the eighteen-forties. It seems not unreasonable to assume that this intimate garment was the origin of the later *maillot* or tights, so that it is no exaggeration to state that the evolution of that article of dress permitted a change in the art of dancing as did the invention of gunpowder on warfare.[2]

Noverre's desire for the abolition of *paniers* had been anticipated in 1734 by Marie Sallé, who appeared in London in a ballet entitled *Pygmalion*, "without paniers, petticoat, and bodice, her hair loose and without any ornament on her head: she was dressed only in a single muslin robe which was draped about her in the manner of a Greek statue."[3] If we may trust the evidence of a contemporary print, the upper part of the "robe" was so scanty that it left one breast exposed.

Noverre also protested against the continuing use of the mask:

> Physiognomy . . . is that part of us most necessary to expression. . . . Why conceal it on the stage by a mask . . . a piece of cardboard which ever appears sad and uniform, cold and motionless? Can the passions be revealed and break through the screen which the dancer places between the spectator and himself? . . . A mask of whatever kind is either cold or pleasing, serious or comic, sad or grotesque. The modeller affords it but one permanent and unvarying character.[4]

Masks had been stylized to an almost ritualistic point, even the colours being laid down by tradition: for tritons green and silver; for demons red and silver; for fauns a smoky brown; winds had cheeks permanently distended. Noverre was of opinion that only these last

[1] J.-G. Noverre, *op. cit.*
[2] Cyril W. Beaumont, *Five Centuries of Ballet Design* (London, 1939).
[3] Quoted by C. W. Beaumont, *op. cit.*
[4] J.-G. Noverre, *op. cit.*

should be kept, since it was manifestly impossible for the dancers them-selves to blow out their cheeks.

It was not, however, until twelve years later that one of his disciples, Maximilien Gardel, dared to appear unmasked. This he did in 1772 in the rôle of Apollo in *Castor and Pollux*. The innovation met with the approval of the public, and thenceforward solo dancers abandoned the mask. But it was retained for some years by the *corps de ballet*.

The costume innovations of female dancers anticipated in a curious fashion the general development of fashionable dress. By the end of the eighteenth century *every* woman had abandoned her panniers and was "dressed only in a single muslin robe which was draped about her in the manner of a Greek statue." There was a corresponding revolution in footgear, high-heeled shoes being abandoned for heel-less slippers. The shoes of the *danseuse* at this period closely resembled the shoes worn by women in ordinary life; a whole generation had to elapse before the toes of dancing-shoes were reinforced to make the *pointe* possible.

So flimsy were female garments in the early years of the nineteenth century that, on the stage, the *maillot*—called after Maillot, a costumier at the Opéra, although, as we have seen, he did not invent it—became obligatory. In the States of the Church it was required to be *blue*, lest it should be mistaken for naked flesh, and in France, under the Restoration, the Superintendent of the Royal Theatres, the prudish Viscount Sosthène de la Rochefocauld, tried to have tights replaced by long pantaloons. Public ridicule put an end to this misguided attempt.

Throughout the first quarter of the nineteenth century costume in opera and ballet was increasingly affected by growing knowledge of the dress of distant times and places. In *Aladin; ou la Lampe Merveilleuse*, an opera performed at the Académie Royale de Musique in Paris in 1822, the dancers wore a very reasonable approximation to Indian costumes, except that the women's dresses all had the high waist of the contemporary mode. Operas of which the theme was rather 'long ago' than 'far away' adopted an extraordinary 'Tudorbethan' style of costume, a blend of ruffs, puffed sleeves, and hats resembling those worn at the time of Henry VIII.

It is necessary, however, to distinguish. As Cyril W. Beaumont reminds us, there were three distinct types of ballet:

the serious or noble style; the *demi-caractère*; and the *caractère*—these terms indicating the style of dancing—each having a basically characteristic costume.

The male dancer in the serious style wore a Greek *chiton* of light material, his legs were bare and his feet shod with sandals strapped round the ankle and base of the calf. The *danseuse* was dressed in a filmy robe—sometimes damped to cling to the figure and more clearly reveal its lines—ending midway between the ankle and calf; the feet were enclosed in buskins.

The male dancer in the *demi-caractère* style wore doublet trunks and long hose, evidently inspired by Renaissance fashions, and a flat-brimmed cap adorned with an ostrich feather. Whether this dress was suggested by certain of the costumes designed by Isabey for the Coronation of Napoleon I, or whether it was selected as being a costume at once decorative and allowing full play for movement, it is impossible to say. The *danseuse* wore a theatricalized version of the cylindrical low-necked dress, gathered beneath the breasts, which remained in general use until 1821, but continued to be seen on the stage in ballets for some years later.

The male dancer in the *caractère* style wore a theatricalized version of the open-necked shirt, short coat, and breeches common to village youths, while the *danseuse* wore a similar version of the dress of a contemporary village girl.[1]

It would be impossible to sum up the matter more neatly.

The designer responsible for most of these dresses was Auguste Garnerey, many of whose original sketches are preserved in the Bibliothèque de l'Opéra in Paris. Numerous lithographs after his designs are to be found in many museums and, as they are generally coloured, give a very good idea of the dresses worn by dancers in the third decade of the nineteenth century. Garnerey became designer of costumes at the Opéra in 1819. He died comparatively young, in 1824, but during the intervening period he dominated the scene by the fertility of his invention and by his capacity for assimilating the new learning about costume with the style of his time.

After his success as the designer for *Aladin* he turned to the old story of *Cendrillon*. It was, says Carlos Fischer, the "current model" of fashionable women. This theatrical costume was also *un costume de ville*. In its details it was Renaissance, but Romantic-Renaissance, *la*

---

[1] Beaumont, *op. cit.*

Renaissance troubadour, in the taste of the moment—that is, in the taste of the early eighteen-twenties. However, for the ballet in *Olimpie, Tragédie lyrique* he reverted to the modes of ancient Greece.

Garnerey was succeeded at the Opéra by Fragonard—not the famous Fragonard but his son, Alexandre-Evariste, who was responsible for the costumes for a couple of years before being succeeded in his turn by Hippolyte Lecomte. Fragonard was particularly successful with his Oriental designs for *Zémire et Azor.* Hippolyte Lecomte, on the other hand, was all for the Middle Ages and Early Renaissance, as seen through the eyes of the subjects of Charles X. His designs for *Guillaume Tell,* performed in Paris in 1829, show the characters in the 'correct' costumes of the Swiss cantons.

In 1831 Lecomte was followed by Paul Lormier, one of his pupils, who held office until 1887. He helped Eugène Lami with the costumes for the ballet in Auber's *Gustave III.* He was more conscientious than inspired, and his excessive zeal for historical accuracy in the costumes of the *figurantes* threw into even sharper relief the strange convention of the *tutu* for the female dancers. The costume of male dancers need hardly detain us at this period. The success of *danseuses* like Taglioni, Grisi, and Fanny Elssler relegated them to a very minor position.

Prominent among the artists working for the Opéra in the reign of Louis-Philippe was G. Lepaulle. His costumes for *Robert le Diable,* produced in 1831, were very well received, the subject itself being very much to the taste of the period. Some of his designs for *Guillaume Tell* show an extraordinary mixture of the slashed sleeves of Renaissance costume and the military uniforms of his own day.

He was followed by Louis Boulanger, whose most successful effort was to design the costumes for *La Esméralda,* produced in 1836. Boulanger was a great admirer of Victor Hugo, and there are still preserved in the Musée Victor Hugo in the Place des Vosges numerous watercolours painted by him for the costumes in *Hernani, Lucrezia Borgia,* and other works by the King of the Romantics.

Opera costume continued, like that of the ordinary stage, to evolve steadily in the direction of realism; but ballet costume—at least the costume of the *première danseuse* and the *corps de ballet,* as opposed to the costume of the *figurantes*—became suddenly stereotyped, and this is such a curious phenomenon, and one which had such far-reaching consequences, that it must be considered in some detail.

In 1832 Marie Taglioni appeared in Paris in the title-rôle of *La Sylphide*. The designer of her costume is thought to have been the well-known painter Eugène Lami, and he provided for the *première danseuse* and for the *corps de ballet*, who were all supposed to be fairies, a dress of white muslin or tarlatan, with a tight-fitting bodice, a low *décolletage*, very short sleeves, and a wide skirt reaching half-way down the calf. This was not so much of an innovation at the time as it seems in retrospect, for Taglioni had appeared two years earlier at the King's Theatre, London, as Flore in the ballet *Flore et Zéphire*. It is true that the skirt is adorned, as befits the character, with a number of posies of flowers and that the sleeves are fuller. It is only necessary to compare both these costumes with contemporary fashion-plates to see that the Taglioni costume is simply the fashionable dress of the early eighteen-thirties, but with the skirt somewhat shortened. It was a slight theatricali-zation of ordinary dress, but that is true of ballet costume from the beginning. Why should it have created so much sensation?

The success of Taglioni as La Sylphide was complete. A charming drawing was made of her by A. E. Chalon, and this was reproduced in lithography and widely sold. It came to be accepted as natural that the *première danseuse* should wear just that costume and no other, *regardless of the subject of the ballet*. It is as if some leading actor had made such a success as Hamlet that his costume became stereotyped for *all* leading actors in *all* plays. The tarlatan ballet skirt, which gradually grew shorter and shorter until it resembled a powder-puff, became *de rigueur*, suggestions of place and period being almost entirely confined to the corsage. For, as Cyril W. Beaumont points out,

there were two sides to the Romantic Ballet, not only the region of legend and the mystic realm of sprites, but the world of realism, which latter inspired such ballets as *Esméralda*, *Catarina*, and *Paquita*, which are set respectively in Paris of the Middle Ages, the Abruzzi, and Spain during the French invasion. In this type of ballet the dress had to suggest both period and nationality. . . . But while the main features of the dancer's costume were established, the dancer's *coiffure* followed the prevailing fashion, whatever character she interpreted, and it was the rule rather than the exception for the *ballerina* to wear a diamond crescent or tiara. Ballet-goers saw nothing incongruous in the dancer's representing a simple peasant with her hair elaborately dressed and wearing jewelled bracelets and necklaces in the most fashionable style.[1]

This strange convention, as artificial in its way as that of the Rococo shepherdess of the eighteenth century, persisted until the end of the nineteenth, and was rendered even more strange when the ballet formed part of an opera the characters of which were dressed with an almost pedantic regard for region and period.

During the second half of the nineteenth century it was obvious that many so-called patrons of opera were not interested in music at all. They were only interested in ballet—or, rather, in the *corps de ballet*. They appeared in their boxes only while the ballet was in progress, and spent the rest of the evening behind the scenes flirting with the *danseuses*. It became almost a social necessity for a member of *la jeunesse dorée* to 'keep' a ballet-girl, who was known, rather surprisingly, as his *rat*. This fact of social history would be outside the scope of our present study were it not for its influence on ballet costume, which in the second half of the century became frankly erotic.

The same tendency was, to a lesser degree, visible in England, but it was Italy that led the way. Even

the Scala at Milan became the centre of the spectacular . . . ballets inaugurated by Luigi Manzotti with his *Excelsior* (1881), *Amor* (1886), and *Sport* (1897), which were not ballets in the present understanding of the term, but mimed episodes varied with danced *ensembles* and stupendous processions of supers, often accompanied by horses and elephants. Manzotti's principal designer was Alfredo Edel, whose costumes were pretty-pretty, fanciful versions of contemporary or historical dress. Animals, vegetables, insects, flowers, birds, reptiles, jewels—there was nothing which the ingenious designer could not translate into terms of costume for ballet.[2]

In a word, these so-called ballets were very much like the spectacular revues put on in modern times by the Folies-Bergère and the Casino de Paris.

[1] Beaumont, *op. cit.*, p. 21.   [2] Beaumont, *op. cit.*, p. 21.

Costume designs by Auguste Garnerey
for the ballet Aladin

Mlle Noblet in the ballet Cendrillon

lotta Grisi and Jules Perrat
the ballet La Esméralda

nilwarth 1831

Zoë Beaupré as Queen Elizabeth, 1831

Joan of Arc

Tristan and Isolde, 1865

RIGHT *Mlle Bréval of the Paris Op*
as Brunnhilde, 1

V.A.M.

of about 1860

of about

1890

Ballet costumes

of 1885

Ballet costume, c. *1860*

Ballet girl 'off duty,' c. *1840*

of c. *1870*

of c. *1890*

A ballet in progress
Punch, *1879*

of c. *1870*

of c. *1890*

Pantomime costumes for Robinson Crusoe

Robinson Crusoe, c. *1880*

Man Friday and Mrs Crusoe, 1882

The Sisters Levey in their Ostrich Dance, 1894

Miss St Cyr, 1894

In London the Alhambra, from 1878 to 1911, and the Empire Theatre, from 1887 to 1914, adopted a similar policy. The principal designer at the Empire was C. Wilhelm. His real name was Pitcher, but he was neither the first nor the last to believe that in the British theatre a foreign name had a certain prestige. A large number of his designs is preserved in the Victoria and Albert Museum, and all of them have charm. They represent ballet-girls (or, as we would say, chorus-girls) dressed as goldfish, swallows, flowers, fruit (one of the designs is a "Costume for a Lemon"), butterflies, pieces of Dresden china, etc. He was particularly successful in his ballet *Les Papillons*, presented at the Empire Theatre in 1901, in transforming male dancers into grasshoppers, but the main interest lay in the female costumes, and these were frankly designed to reveal as much of the figure as the law allowed.

Even more frankly erotic were the designs by Comelli, whose work might be described as an exploitation of the ample thighs (covered with pink tights, over which were worn open-work stockings) of the show-girls of the period. There is a certain stylized *bravura* about his drawings, but the emotion they tried to provoke in the audience was hardly an aesthetic one.

It was in reaction against this kind of entertainment, which should not rightly have been called ballet at all, and in revolt against the fossilized conventions of the classical ballet at the end of the nineteenth century, that Isadora Duncan launched her protest and Diaghilev staged his revolt.

CHAPTER NINE

THE TWENTIETH CENTURY

REALISM had been the watchword of all theatrical reformers since the last quarter of the eighteenth century. They were hampered, as we have seen, by their mere lack of knowledge; it was not until much later that they had enough material to work on. Gradually, however, the information accumulated. The nineteenth century, for good or ill, was historically-minded, more historically-minded than any age before it in world history. Stage designers, and even audiences, were becoming increasingly 'period-conscious.'

We have noted what pains Charles Kean took to give his productions of Shakespeare the right 'period flavour,' even when it was extremely doubtful which particular period Shakespeare had had in mind. The tendency was carried still further in the eighteen-seventies by the remarkable theatre group known as the Meiningers. Saxe-Meiningen was a small German Principality—its capital had only 8000 inhabitants —but its ruler, Duke George II, was a man of artistic tastes and with a passion for the theatre. He was also a practising artist. Dissatisfied with the meaningless jumble of supposedly historical costumes and scenery and with the thousand and one theatrical conventions carried over from the eighteenth century, he set himself to reform the staging of plays from top to bottom. He himself designed both costumes and settings, making every effort to draw upon authentic sources. He even had an armourer on duty in the theatre, and each actor was given written instructions for the wearing of his costume.

Having perfected their productions in their own capital, the Meiningers set out on a tour of Europe. On May 1, 1874, they appeared in Berlin and were received with the utmost enthusiasm. In the following year they were in Vienna and Budapest, and between 1874 and 1890 they performed more than 2500 times, reaching as far as London, Amsterdam, Copenhagen, Stockholm, Basle, Warsaw, St Petersburg, Moscow, and Odessa.

"The company," says Lee Simonson,

became the first theatre of Europe, a school of the theatre for every theatrical centre. None escaped its influence. Every tradition of routine repertory based on opera was discredited, and a method of bringing plays to life on the boards was everywhere recognized as nothing less than a new art. . . . No important director since the duke's time has failed to be a disciple of one aspect or another of his theories and his practice.[1]

It so happened that two men who were afterwards to play an important part in theatrical production came under the influence of the Meiningers at the most impressionable and formative period of their lives. One of these was André Antoine, who had seen them perform in Brussels; the other was Constantin Stanislavsky, who, while still an amateur, had seen them in Moscow in 1885. In 1887 Antoine founded the Théâtre Libre in Paris to proclaim the new doctrine of stage naturalism. Everything had to be real, even to a joint of meat on the table, and the plays he selected were of the 'realist' school, dealing for the most part with modern life. His innovations are of more interest to the historian of stage décor than to the historian of stage costume. The costumes, indeed, were simply those of every day.

Stanislavsky was in Paris in 1892, and afterwards admitted how much he owed to the experimental work being carried on at this time in the French capital, not only by Antoine at the Théâtre Libre, but also by Paul Fort at the Théâtre d'Art, which in that very year became the Théâtre de l'Œuvre. Stanislavsky returned to Russia, and in 1897 had that famous all-night conversation with Vladimir Nemirovich-Danchenko which resulted in the formation of the Art Theatre of Moscow.

[1] Lee Simonson, *The Stage is Set* (New York, 1932).

The original doctrine of the Moscow Art Theatre was naturalism in its most extreme form, and Stanislavsky's triumphs in this direction, his creation of an acting ensemble, as opposed to the system of 'star-and-super,' his attempts to reproduce on the stage the actual conditions of life, are part of theatre history, but it must be admitted that he pushed matters to an extreme. As Theodore Komisarjevsky tells us,

> In its first production the Moscow Art Theatre . . . slavishly followed the traditions of the Meininger, transplanting them on to Russian soil. On the opening night, in the production of the poetical and historical Russian play *Tzar Fyodor Ivanovitch*, the costumes of the Tzar, of the boyards, and of the Moscow people were exact replicas of historical documents and made as far as possible of the genuine old materials. The long bejewelled brocade coats of the boyards had fur collars and were lined throughout with fur, which made them so heavy that it seemed almost impossible for the actors to breathe, let alone move in them. . . . In the production of *Julius Caesar* the stage was so filled with brass armour, helmets, weapons, ample togas, and various minute details of costume and properties, that Shakespeare's play was completely drowned. The heights of naturalism, however, were reached when the Moscow Art Theatre presented Leo Tolstoy's *The Power of Darkness* and Gorky's *The Lower Depths*, which latter production was afterwards copied by Max Reinhardt in Berlin.[1]

The same tendencies could be seen all over Europe: in the productions of Brahm in Germany, of David Belasco in the United States, and of Sir Herbert Tree in London.

Meanwhile there had been a revolt against realism. Komisarjevsky, the distinguished 'man of the theatre' from whom we have already quoted, was the first to point out the importance of the Russian contribution to this movement:

> The reaction against naturalism in costume and production in Russia at the end of the nineteenth century was started by a rich business man, Savva Mamontov, who ran an operatic theatre in Moscow called "The Private Opera." He engaged artists to design the settings and costumes for his theatre who assisted his new movement by ignoring 'reproduction' and historical accuracy, making only artistic compositions of forms and colour. . . . Costume, in the hands of these painters, who were influenced more by the world of art and poetry of the past than by history or the actual conditions of life, became a work of pictorial art. . . . In order to achieve total harmony with the décor the artists employed by Mamontov

[1] Theodore Komisarjevsky, *The Costume of the Theatre* (London, 1931).

frequently had complete costumes made of hand-painted designs, and furs and armour were often painted on cloth and canvas as substitutes for the real materials. . . . The stage work of most of these painters was inspired by the primitive Russian paintings, the antique ikons and frescoes, and by the popular coloured prints and other decorative works of ancient peasant art.[1]

Something very similar was happening in France. Paul Fort, in Paris, had never subscribed to Antoine's doctrine; indeed, his Théâtre d'Art had been founded in opposition to the Théâtre Libre. He strove to simplify stage scenery, to make it evocative rather than descriptive, to make the costumes harmonize with it, and at the same time, by different colour schemes in the different acts, to reinforce the mood of the play. Maeterlinck's *Pelléas et Mélisande* gave him his opportunity, for this was a play which it would obviously have been absurd to present in the conventions of naturalism.

In opera a similar development was taking place, at first only in theory. Adolphe Appia, dissatisfied with the staging and costuming of Wagner at Bayreuth, wrote a pamphlet suggesting improvements, and in 1899 followed this up with a monumental work, *Die Musik und die Inscenierung*, in which he tackled the whole problem of stage production. His protest was not directed so much against realism as against the false realism common in operatic production at that time, when a painted perspective scene might have real or imitation leaves attached to strips of netting and hung from the flies. He declared that when it was desired to represent a forest, as in the second act of *Siegfried*, it was not necessary to give the spectator the illusion of a forest, but of a man in the atmosphere of a forest. The silhouetted trunks of a few trees (the improvement of stage lighting having now made such effects possible) were all that was required. The costumes too should be drastically simplified, suggesting a period rather than seeking to reproduce 'historical' costume in any detail. Appia's work had little effect on stage production at the time, but it served as a rallying-ground for those in the early twentieth century who were seeking to restore to the theatre the hieratic quality which it had once possessed and which the modern theatre so plainly lacked.

[1] Komisarjevsky, *op. cit.*

Prominent among these was Gordon Craig. He was the son of E. W. Godwin, who in the seventies and eighties had shown his ability both as an architect and as a stage designer, and of the famous actress Ellen Terry. Through his mother's influence he was able to put his theories into practice in several productions in London: *Acis and Galatea, The Masque of Love,* and Ibsen's *Pretenders.* He was less successful with Ibsen's *Rosmersholm* in which Eleanora Duse appeared in 1906, for this was a play that did not lend itself in any way to Craig's methods. Four years later Stanislavsky, who was himself outgrowing his early passion for realism, invited Craig to Moscow to stage *Hamlet* at the Art Theatre.

Craig's ideas had very much more influence on stage scenery than on stage costume. Here the liberating influence came largely from Russia itself. Vronbel and Konstantin Korovin based themselves on popular art, and Nicholas Sapounov and Serge Soudeikin derived inspiration from medieval ikons, tapestries, old Russian china figures, and the like. Their influence, however, might have been confined to Russia itself if it had not been for Diaghilev.

Nevertheless, the movement did not begin with him. It arose, almost by chance, among a group of young men who had been fellow-pupils in a private school in St Petersburg between 1880 and 1890. This group of friends, under the leadership of Alexandre Benois, formed a kind of club—oddly enough, they called themselves "the Pickwickians" —and before long were joined by a young Jew whose name was Léon Rosenberg, who later took his maternal grandfather's name of Bakst. The only member with any theatrical background was Benois. His mother was the daughter of the architect of the Imperial Theatre and granddaughter of a famous composer and conductor.

An important member of the group was Dima Filosofov, who was to play no direct part in subsequent developments; "but he is important, if only because he had a provincial cousin at school in distant Perm in the Urals, on the borders of Asia. In August 1890 this cousin, having finished school, came to St Petersburg and through Filosofov made the acquaintance of the 'Pickwickians.' This cousin was Serge Diaghilev."[1]

[1] Prince Peter Lieven, *The Birth of Ballets-Russes* (London, 1936).

At first he was of little account in the circle. He had really come to St Petersburg to study music, but soon turned to an appreciation of painting. When *Mir Iskustva* (*The World of Art*) was founded in 1898 it was his organizing ability that made its first exhibition a success. *Mir Iskustva* was a society and a journal, the first number of which was issued in 1900. It had immense influence, grouping around itself all that was vital at the time in Russian painting. Prince Serge Wolkonsky, the newly appointed Director of the Imperial Theatre, made Diaghilev a junior assistant, and soon after Benois was allowed to produce an opera at the Hermitage Theatre and Bakst was commissioned to design the costumes for a play.

Bakst also designed the costumes for a projected production of Delibes's ballet *Sylvia*, and this might perhaps be described as the most important theatrical production *that never happened*. Intrigues against the new men resulted in the dismissal of Diaghilev from his official post.

> The possibility of creative theatrical work in Russia on the scale he wanted was denied him for ever. We, however, must remember that, but for the *Sylvia* 'scandal,' Diaghilev would probably have remained in Russia, and the *Ballets-Russes* perhaps would never have come into existence.
>
> [In 1907, however] in St Petersburg there occurred what must be counted the first step in the direction of the *Ballets-Russes*—and Diaghilev had no part in it. It was Benois who was responsible for a production of *Le Pavillon d'Armide*, a project he had long had in mind, and for which he designed the scenery and costumes. It was notable in many ways; for the engagement of Michael Fokine as choreographer, and for another event which must excite the imagination of all *balletomanes*. One day, during the rehearsals, Fokine remarked to Benois:
>
> "I have in mind a pupil who is just finishing at the school. He is very talented. Do you think we might invent some part for him?"
>
> "Who is he?" asked Benois.
>
> "You don't know him. His name is Vazlav Nijinsky."[1]

Le Pavillon d'Armide was an artistic success even with those who did not realize with what taste and skill Benois had, in his scenery and costumes, evoked the very spirit of the *Grand Siècle*. The Russian authorities continued, however, to throw every possible difficulty in

[1] Lieven, *op. cit.*

the way; and the thoughts of the *Mir Iskustva* group began to turn towards the West.

In 1908 Diaghilev presented at the Opéra in Paris his first theatrical venture—*Boris Godounov*, with Chaliapin in the chief part. It was well received, but rather by a cultivated *élite* than by the general public. But in the following year at the Châtelet Theatre *Prince Igor* took Paris by storm. The scenery and costumes by Roerich, with their sombre yet brilliant colouring, were something that Western Europe had never seen before. Nijinsky in *Le Pavillon d'Armide* evoked the utmost enthusiasm; so did Benois's décor and costumes for *Les Sylphides*, in which he returned to the long *tutu* as it had been worn by Taglioni, and evoked the whole spirit of the sentimental Romanticism of the eighteen-thirties. *Cléopâtre*, in which Nijinsky and Karsavina danced together, proved the greatest financial success. Bakst's scenery—according to Benois's generous tribute, "was rather hurriedly and sketchily executed, but the conception was good and the colour, rose-granite and dark violet, was beautiful. Against this weird, truly southern, oppressively warm background the purple costumes glistened richly." Bakst had struck his characteristic note.

In the following year he designed the costumes for *L'Oiseau de Feu*, although the scenery was by Golovin. But Bakst's greatest success in the Paris season of 1910 was in *Carnaval*. This was danced on an empty stage without any scenery at all, except for blue hangings with a frieze, and the costumes, in Biedermeyer style of ordinary calico, made all the more impact. For another successful production, *Giselle*, the décor and costumes were designed by Benois. But the high-water mark of the *Ballets-Russes* this year was undoubtedly *Schéhérazade*.

This has long been considered to be Bakst's supreme achievement. Once more we must fall back on Benois's appreciation, the more generous from the fact that the idea of the ballet had been largely his and that his name did not even appear on the programme:

> To Bakst really belongs the credit of creating *Schéhérazade* as a spectacle—and an astonishing, I should say, unique spectacle. . . . The emerald shades of these awnings, hangings, walls and throne, the deepness of the night which pierces the

Costume design by Léon Bakst
for The Sleeping Princess, *1921*

barred windows opening on the oppressive harem garden, these piles of embroidered cushions and mattresses . . . these half-naked dancers . . . all these things produced a complete and instantaneous charm. . . . I have never before seen such a harmony of colour on the stage, such a fine and complex orchestration of colour.[1]

"A fine and complex orchestration of colour." That was the point. After *Schéhérazade* stage costume and décor could never be quite the same again. Its influence was seen, not only in ballet, but in every kind of theatrical production in which there was any exotic or historical element. Nor was its effect confined to the theatre. It created a new style in women's dress—in spite of the protests of Paul Poiret that his designs were uninfluenced by the Russian Ballet. It spread to interior decoration: the brilliant hangings and cushions of Bakst's harem were copied in many a drawing-room. It changed people's colour-sense overnight.

But the frank voluptuousness of *Schéhérazade* was not Bakst's only note. There was also the seductive cruelty of *Cléopâtre*, the virginal innocence of *Le Spectre de la Rose*, the tongue-in-cheek Romanticism of *Carnaval*, the wilful *naïveté* of *Narcisse*, the primitive savagery of *Tamar*. In all these, as in *Le Dieu Bleu* and *L'Après-midi d'un Faune*, Bakst demonstrated the astonishing virtuosity of his handling of colour and the curious directness and violence of his appeal to the senses. He remains, in general estimation and in actual fact, the most important of the stage designers employed for the *Ballets-Russes*.

We must not, however, forget the admirable costumes designed by Benois for *Petrushka*, nor Boris Anisfeldt's work for *Sadko*, nor that of Soudeikin for *Salomé* in the 1913 season. For *Le Coq d'Or* produced in 1914 the designs were allotted to Gontcharova, whose husband, Larionov, worked for Diaghilev later. Another Russian painter, Doboujinsky, was responsible for the scenery and costumes for *Midas*, a ballet which had little success and was never revived.

The First World War and the Russian Revolution cut Diaghilev off from his base: the source from which he had drawn his dancers, his choreographers, and his decorators. Prince Peter Lieven sums up the situation as follows:

[1] Lieven, *op. cit.*

The united group, with whose members Diaghilev had reached maturity, whose leader he was, no longer existed. To remain the protagonist of all that was progressive in art he had to go and seek for "advancedness," had to attract to his service collaborators who had already had the hall-mark of *le dernier cri*. Before, he himself had created a revolution; now, he had to search for one and follow in its wake. Picasso, Dérain, Marie Laurencin, Braque, Juan Gris, Pruna, Utrillo, and Chirico—all these painters had created a name for themselves independently of Diaghilev.[1]

Diaghilev made several attempts after the war to return to the past, notably in the 1921 London production of *The Sleeping Princess*. He had wanted it staged by Benois, but Benois was unable to escape from Russia, and Diaghilev had to fall back on Bakst. Bakst produced a magnificent series of designs, but the London production was a financial failure, and at the end of the season all the scenery and costumes had to be sold by auction.

In Russia, after the Revolution, the extreme Left in art found itself, like the extreme Left in politics, suddenly in power. Realism, which had depicted too faithfully the *bourgeois* life against which every tendency in Russia was now in violent revolt, was discredited. Anything revolutionary, or merely different, was, for the moment, welcome to the authorities, who, although under the stress of famine, foreign invasion, and civil war, kept the theatres open. Even ballet, that most artificial of Court entertainments, continued. And Russia was fortunate in possessing men of the theatre who, before the Revolution, had been consistently pursuing new methods of presentation.

The new school was headed by Tairov and Meyerhold, who sought to make the theatre frankly theatrical. Their chief influence was on décor. 'Constructivism,' the term generally used to cover their activities, stripped the stage bare of all accessories and filled it with mechanical structures, bare staircases, trestles, terraces, and inclined planes. In costume it tended to an extreme stylization, as in those dresses made for *Phedra* at the Kamerny Theatre, Moscow, where the form of Greek helmets and tunics was suggested rather than copied. It sought to harmonize scenery and costumes, as when, in Tairov's

[1] Lieven, *op. cit.*

Romeo and Juliet, the strange foldings and flutings of the background were continued in the costumes.

For some tastes, however, even Meyerhold and Tairov were insufficiently revolutionary. What was really wanted, it was thought, was an abolition of all the conventions of the theatre and a return to the primitiveness of "three planks and a passion." Eisenstein (later to become world famous for his films) founded his Russian reputation as the theatre director of the Proletkult. His stage was a simple platform with no décor at all, and his actors were dressed as clowns or acrobats.

Many elements of Russian life that had been suppressed under the Tsars now flowed into the theatre, in particular the influence of the Jews. No less than three Jewish theatres were supported by the State. The Habima Players are now world famous, but in Moscow in the twenties the National Jewish Theatre, playing not in Hebrew but in Yiddish, was more important. Its members were at first amateurs, but, under their extremely able *régisseur* Granovsky, they soon made a reputation. Granovsky employed Chagall as his decorator, and this remarkable artist at once established a style which, combined with the Constructivism of Rabinovitch, set the tone for all subsequent productions.

Throughout the first ten years of the Revolutionary period the theatre in Russia, in spite of its bewildering variety, was held together as a unity by its consistent glorification of the new order of things. However, at the end of the twenties, a kind of neo-Romanticism set in, and with the advent of Stalin this was transformed into a positively *bourgeois* attitude to art, hostile to experiment and to the work of 'advanced' painters and decorators. The wheel had come full circle, and many of those who had been most revolutionary in the twenties fell from favour. Meyerhold committed suicide.

The revolt against realism had manifested itself, independently, all over Europe. In Germany the movement may be summed up in the career of Max Reinhardt. Beginning as an actor in the ultra-realistic Freie Bühne of Otto Brahm, he soon branched out on his own as a producer, first in art cabarets and later in the legitimate theatre. Reinhardt was essentially an eclectic. He was indifferent to style as such and sought only to reinforce what might be called the *dominant flavour* of a play. At the Kleines Theater, Berlin, he produced Gorky's *Nachtasyl* (*The Lower Depths*) in an extremely realistic manner, the actors being clothed in dirty rags, but in *A Midsummer Night's Dream*, put on at the Neues Theater in 1905, he blended realism and fantasy. He believed in employing as decorators and designers of costumes men who were not primarily scenic artists. For the costumes of *Minna von Barnhelm* he employed the veteran illustrator Menzel, famous for his devotion to historical exactitude; but for his first *Merchant of Venice* he brought in Emil Orlik, and for *Œdipus and the Sphinx* Alfred Roller. Lovis Corinth and Karl Walser both worked for him during his first season at the Deutsches Theater, and in his production of Offenbach's *Orphée* we see for the first time the hand of Ernst Stern, a brilliantly imaginative artist who was to become Reinhardt's favourite decorator.

Reinhardt's real originality was in his staging, which is outside the scope of the present study. He put on *Œdipus Rex* in a circus in Berlin and staged *The Miracle* at Olympia in London. *Everyman* was presented for the first time in the Domplatz against the Baroque façade of Salzburg Cathedral. His costumes, however, went no further than a certain stylization, nor is it easy to see how they could have done otherwise.

One of the first of the important exhibitions of stage design that have since become so frequent was held at the Zürich Kunstgewerbemuseum in April 1914. Appia and Gordon Craig were frankly acknowledged as the leaders of the modern movement, and the designs of Emil Orlik were given due prominence. Among other, mostly German, designers whose costume sketches were shown were Franz Nitsche, of Leipzig, Rochus Gliese, of Berlin, Koloman Moser, of Vienna, and H. C. Forestier, of Geneva.

Some of the most daring experiments in costume design were made in the twenties at the Bauhaus, Dessau, that laboratory for research into the fundamental principles of all the arts. Oskar Schlemmer devised a costume made of coils of wire projecting from black tights for a female dancer in the *Triadischen Ballet*. He restored the mask in various forms, sometimes reducing the human head to a metal sphere; he sought by means of vertical white tapes on a black costume to assimilate the human body to a spinning top. In the *Kastenpromenade* of the *Exzentrisches Ballet* the dancers wear costumes that look like anticipations of space-suits.

There were many good designers in Germany in the decade following the war. Many of them followed Reinhardt not so much in his individual development as in his eclecticism, his willingness to use all manners from complete realism to extreme stylization so long as the manner chosen fitted the mood of the play. Hans Wilderman, of Breslau, and Hans Strohbach, at Cologne, used many styles, but with a leaning towards the grandeur of the Baroque. In the late twenties the most revolutionary of German producers was Piscator, who in Berlin used a method of staging that incorporated both the circus and the film. His costumes were non-naturalistic, but did not reach the extreme of those invented for the Bauhaus.

The universal interest in Germany in décor and costume at this period was shown by the ambitious Theatre Exhibition at Magdeburg in 1927. But all these activities and all theatrical experiment were brought to an end by the advent of Hitler. Ashley Dukes, writing for *The Theatre Arts Monthly* early in 1934, reported on the state of the German theatre after the Nazis took over. It was a record of complete collapse. All the leading dramatists—Wedekind, Werfel, Toller, Hasenclever, even Gerhart Hauptmann—were in disgrace; so were the designers of sets and costumes, for they were all tainted with *Kultur-Bolshevismus*. Max Reinhardt, as a Jew, was deprived of his control of his theatres, but this was, perhaps, no great matter as he had already transferred much of his activity to Vienna and Salzburg, where, until the Anschluss, he was able to work in peace.

In France the example of Diaghilev in calling in artists who were not (or were not only) stage decorators bore fruit when the State theatres commissioned costumes from men like Maxime Dethomas and Valdo Barbey. The Théâtre des Arts employed Desvallières; the Vieux Colombier, Luc-Albert Moreau and others; the Atelier, Barsacq and Jean-Victor Hugo. Barsacq's style both in décor and costumes is generally formal and austere, but he knows how to seize upon the essentials of an epoch that is neither one nor the other, and he gave to

Jonson's *Volpone* a production that had all the robust extravagance of its epoch. Jean-Victor Hugo's most striking success was with his designs, for the Soirées de Paris, of a play that he had the honesty to call *Roméo et Juliette, Prétexte à mise-en-scène*. The costumes were in black and white and might be described as a fantasia on the theme of the ruff. His more recent work includes designs for *Phèdre, Ruy Blas*, and for a remarkable presentation of *Le Carosse du Saint-Sacrement* at the Perpignan Festival in 1951.

Other French artists who have worked for the stage include Cocteau, Desnoyer, Dignimont, Fernand Léger, Vertés, and Christian Bérard. The last-named was such a stimulating influence in all departments of the decorative arts that it would be strange indeed if he had had no impact on the theatre. He made designs for Molière's *École des Femmes*, produced by Jouvet at the Théâtre de l'Athénée, and for Cocteau's *Rénaud et Armide* at the Comédie-Française. His extraordinary sense of chic was shown in his costumes for *Amphitryon* and *Les Fourberies de Scapin*.

T. S. Eliot's *Murder in the Cathedral* was put on at the Vieux Colombier in 1945 with very successful costumes by L. Gischia. This artist excels in the task of period evocation. His costumes, ranging from *Œdipus* to *Danton*, taking in *Le Cid, Richard II, Ruy Blas*, Musset's *Lorenzaccio*, and Molière's *L'Avare* on the way, show that he is able to suggest the essential flavour of an epoch without ever falling into the pedantry of mere 'historical reconstruction.'

F. Labisse is another artist who is able to present a period long past in his own terms and at the same time to reinforce the author's intentions. He has made designs for plays as different as Obey's *Noé* and Kafka's *Le Procès*. Wakhevitch is as well known for his work at Stratford as for his work in Paris. It is interesting to note that there has recently been, in French productions, a revival of the mask, ranging from Bertholle's stylized creations for the *Agamemnon* of Æschylus to the terrifying realism of J. Vlach's severed head for *Macbeth*.

In Italy before 1914 there was little sign of a break with the traditional method of presenting opera and plays. However, Marinetti, the inventor of Futurism, was in revolt against this as he was in revolt against all traditions. His disciple Bragaglia, shortly after Mussolini's

March on Rome, established his Teatro della Rivoluzione, which would, perhaps, have been Constructivist in its use of machines if the Russians had not already appropriated that particular style. It is hard to find a consistent thread in his work unless it was a protest against the *literary* aspect of drama and against any kind of realism in presentation.

The influence of European developments began to be felt in the United States of America shortly before the First World War. Appia, Craig, Reinhardt—all had their effect on the thinking and practice of American designers. One of the pioneers was Robert Edmond Jones, who, as early as 1915, was simplifying his settings, keeping them light in tone in order to throw up the brilliant orange and yellow of the costumes. Lee Simonson, Joseph Urban, and Norman Bel Geddes experimented with all the new methods of stage production. Most of their innovations were in décor, and so outside the scope of this book, but Robert Edmond Jones made some interesting experiments in showing one age through the eyes of another as when he costumed *Lucrèce* in terms of Renaissance Rome. Somewhat in the same spirit, but much more recently, Valentina provided stylized wigs and Greek dress for Alfred Lunt's production of *Amphitryon 38*. Joseph Urban took advantage of the opportunities offered by the Ziegfeld Follies.

The next generation of stage designers in America included such masters of their craft as Cleon Throckmorton, Mordecai Gorelik, Jo Mielziner, Donald Oenslager, Stewart Chaney (especially in his costumes for *Twelfth Night*, 1940), Aline Bernstein, Woodman Thompson, James Reynolds and Albert Johnson (mostly in revue), and Cecil Smith (ballet and musical comedy). Lemuel Ayres had great success with *Oklahoma!* and *Kiss Me, Kate*. Other leading American stage designers were Nat Karson, Millia Davenport, Lucinda Ballard, Helen Pons, Claude Bragdon, Simon Lissim, and Raoul Pene du Bois.

For the first twenty years of the century England, in spite of the admonitions of Gordon Craig, remained largely outside the European movement. There were, however, individual artists of great talent. One of the most remarkable of these was Charles Ricketts. He was so much in love with the theatre that he frequently made elaborate sketches of costumes for plays which had little or no chance of being presented. As early as 1906 he had decorated *Salome* and *A Florentine Tragedy*, and he followed these with designs for *Don Juan in Hell* and *The Man of Destiny*. It was not until some sixteen years later that the public acclaimed his costumes for *Saint Joan*. Then followed *Henry VIII* and *Macbeth*, but his attempts to re-dress *The Mikado* were less favourably received. His last work was for *Elizabeth of England* in 1929.

Claud Lovat Fraser died in 1921 at a tragically early age, but he made a great impact in the short time at his disposal, and his influence has lasted until to-day. For *As You Like It*, produced at the Lyric Theatre, Hammersmith, in 1920, he designed clothes which were almost pedantically accurate; but in the same year he tackled the scenery and costumes for Nigel Playfair's revival of *The Beggar's Opera*. In these he eliminated all unnecessary detail. As Nigel Playfair tells us:

> Everything in the way of flowered and figured materials was avoided, simply because the designer wanted to create a very clean, hard and unsentimental colour-scheme in keeping with the general character of the play. The broad main lines of the designs—the hoops, wigs, hats, shoes and the very wide-cuffed sleeves, were absolutely correct by historical examples; but once he had established the accurate effect, the designer allowably gave his fancy free play.[1]

Fraser also designed the dresses for Pergolesi's *La Serva Padrona*, but it was his work for *The Beggar's Opera* that established his reputation and contributed much to the phenomenal success of the play.

Other designers who worked for Playfair were George Sheringham, whose costumes and settings for *The Duenna* evoked the atmosphere of eighteenth-century Spain; Norman Wilkinson, who was responsible for *The Rivals* and *Lionel and Clarissa*; and Doris Zinkeisen, who was chosen to dress that production of *The Way of the World* which is remembered in theatrical history for the performance of Edith Evans as Millamant. Doris Zinkeisen also designed some striking costumes for *The Insect Play*, which Playfair put on at the Regent Theatre. For *Polly* Playfair called in the famous painter William Nicholson. He employed other artists such as Michael Sevier and John Armstrong, and nearly all of those to whom he thus gave a chance justified his talent-spotting by having successful careers as stage designers.

[1] Nigel Playfair, *Costume at the Lyric Theatre; Robes of Thespis* (London, 1928).

Another impresario who did much to encourage the scenic artist was Barry Jackson, in spite of his liking for 'Shakespeare in modern dress.' His principal designer at the Birmingham Repertory Theatre was Paul Shelving, who, for years, faced the problem of decorating a new play every fortnight. In Barry Jackson's own opinion the high-water mark of his achievement was the setting and costumes of Shaw's *Back to Methuselah*. He was able to fantasticate costume without losing its essential line, as in his designs for Lord Dunsany's *The Queen's Enemies* and Molière's *Le Bourgeois Gentilhomme*.

George Harris found scope for his talents in a wide variety of plays. Aubrey Hammond, one of the best of the scenic designers of the twenties, decorated, among many other plays, *The Man with a Load of Mischief* and *The Circle of Chalk*. At the Abbey Theatre, Dublin, one of the most successful designers was Norah McGuinness, especially with her imaginative reconstructions of ancient Irish dress for W. B. Yeats's *Deirdre*.

Modern plays written in the realistic idiom gave very little scope for artistic creation, and for a time it seemed that décor would pass from the hands of the stage designer into those of the interior decorator and house-furnisher. A similar tendency was manifest in stage costume. The actors' clothes were made by fashionable tailors and the actresses' by the leading couturiers. It was the lighter stage which often gave the designer his chance, and an enlightened producer of revues and musical plays like C. B. Cochran did more than most theatrical managers to bring new talent into the theatre. He employed Oliver Messel to design a few masks, then a complete revue, and finally the whole setting and costumes for the magnificent revival of *Helen!* Messel has since gone on to demonstrate the range of his talent in such different productions as *Tough at the Top* (one of the last of the Cochran shows) and *Ring round the Moon*. For other productions Cochran employed Doris Zinkeisen, one of the most uniformly successful designers of revue costumes, Cathleen Mann, Rex Whistler, and others. Gladys Calthrop designed some excellent 'period' dresses for Noel Coward's *Conversation Piece* under Cochran's management.

The reopening of Sadler's Wells and the building up of a permanent company for opera and ballet resulted in a whole new field being opened to stage designers. William Chappell was responsible for some admirable sets and costumes for *Coppélia*; John Piper, who had already made his name as a painter, designed *The Quest*; he has done much excellent work since, especially, perhaps, for *Billy Budd*. Among recent work may be mentioned his imaginative costumes for *A Midsummer Night's Dream* as an opera. Leslie Hurry caught the public attention with *Le Lac des Cygnes*, and Hugh Stevenson with *The Gods Go A-begging*. Hurry's later work includes the setting and costumes for *Tamburlaine* and *The Duchess of Malfi*.

Cecil Beaton, who has made several reputations—as a photographer, as a writer, and as a decorative artist—is a virtuoso of what might be called 'period chic.' His work for the revival of *Lady Windermere's Fan* at the Haymarket contributed largely to the success of the play. More recently his costumes for *My Fair Lady* were much admired.

After the war the rise of a drama not so exclusively concerned with ordinary life offered new scope for designers, which was eagerly seized by men like Roger Furse (*Venus Observed*), Oliver Messel (*The Lady's not for Burning* and *Ring round the Moon*), Edward Delaney (*King's Rhapsody*), by Sophie Fedorovitch (*The Winter's Tale*) and the ladies who called themselves Motley (*Richard of Bordeaux*). An artist who came to the theatre from other fields is Osbert Lancaster, whose strong sense of period with just a hint of caricature soon placed him in the front rank of theatrical designers. Yet another is Michael Ayrton, well known as painter, critic, and broadcaster, who in 1951 made a sensation with his work for Purcell's *The Faery Queen*. At Stratford, during the 1948 Shakespeare Festival, James Bailey created even more by devising Victorian settings and costumes for *Hamlet*: the King in side-whiskers and Ophelia in a crinoline. Alan Barlow struck an original note with his pastiche of Rowlandson in the Old Vic production of *She Stoops to Conquer*.

It is impossible, within the compass of the present work, to make any comprehensive list of British stage designers. The play producer to-day can call upon a bewildering variety of talent. In addition to those already mentioned, those who have done excellent work in the theatre within recent years include Reece Pemberton, Tanya Moiseiwitch,

Costume design by Alexandre Benois for Nijinsky
Armide, *St Petersburg, 1907*

Costume design by Léon Bakst for Le Bouffon Russe
The Sleeping Princess, *1921*

Costume design for Anna Pavlova
by Natalia Gontcharova

*Costume designs for ballet
by Andreenko, 1925*

"LA SERVA PADRONA"
"THE MAID TURNED MISTRESS"
LYRIC OPERA HOUSE,
HAMMERSMITH.
29th Jany: 1919.
VESPONE. 2nd Dress.
(Mr. Tom Reynolds).
C. LOVAT FRASER. 1919.

Costume design by Claud Lovat Fraser for La Serva Padrona, *1919*

Hermione

Leontes

ostume designs by Charles Ricketts for The Winter's Tale

Costume design by Doris Zinkeisen
for The Insect Play, *1923*

Costume design by Simon Lissim
for La Prochaine, *1937*

Costume design by Ernst Stern for
Le Bourgeois Gentilhomme, *1912*

The Importance of being Earnest!

Gwendolyn Act II
Iris Barker.

July 1930.

Michael Weight.

Costume design for The Importance of Being Earnest
by Michael Weight, 1930

Costume design for The Duenna
by George Sheringham, 1924

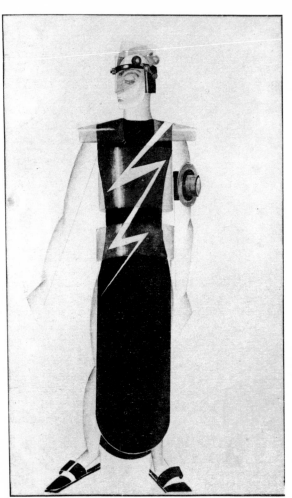

Two costume designs by Alexandra Exter

*Costume designs
by Jean-Victor Hugo
for*
Roméo et Juliette

Costume design by E. Prampolini for La Nuit Métallique

Two dancers in the ballet
Tempo Universel
Monte Carlo, 1959

Performance of
Romain Rolland's
Carnaval *at the*
Russian Propaganda
Theatre

*Costumes for ballet by
Oskar Schlemmer*

*Costume in Handel's
Julius Caesar
Darmstadt, 1927*

*Costumes for ballet by
Oskar Schlemmer*

Leonard Rosoman, Osborne Robinson, Robert Medley, Nicholas Georgiades, Franco Zeffirelli, Anthony Holland, Peter Rice, Audrey Cruddas, Felix Kelly, Lila de Nobili, Sean Kenny, Alix Stone, and Desmond Heeley.

The critic looking back on the long history of costume in the theatre can at least assure himself that *that* department of the decorative arts is in a flourishing condition not only in these islands and in America, but all over the world.

SELECT BIBLIOGRAPHY

GENERAL

BOEHN, M. VON: *Das Bühnenkostüm* (Berlin, 1921).

CHENEY, SHELDON: *The Theatre: Three Thousand Years of Drama, Acting and Stagecraft* (London, 1929).

DUBECH, L.: *Histoire générale illustrée du théâtre* (5 vols., Paris, 1931–34).

FREEDLEY, G., AND REEVES, J. A.: *A History of the Theatre* (New York, 1941).

GREGOR, J.: *Weltgeschichte des Theaters* (Zürich, 1934).

—— *Das Bühnenkostüm* (Vienna, 1925).

JULLIEN, A.: *Histoire du costume au théâtre* (Paris, 1880).

KOMISARJEVSKY, T.: *The Costume of the Theatre* (London, 1931).

MANTZIUS, K.: *A History of Theatrical Art* (6 vols., London, 1903–21; New York, 1937).

NICOLL, ALLARDYCE: *The Development of the Theatre* (fourth edition, London, 1958).

1: DRESSING UP TO DANCE

BÉDOUIN, J.-L.: *Les Masques* (Paris, 1961).

BUDGE, E. A. WALLIS: *Osiris and the Egyptian Resurrection*, chapter on "Shrines, Miracle Plays, and Mysteries" (London, 1911).

CORNFORD, F. M.: *The Origin of Attic Comedy* (London, 1914).

GREGOR, J.: *Masks of the World* (London, 1936–37).

HAMBLY, W. D.: *Tribal Dancing and Social Development* (London, 1926).

HARTLAND, E. S.: *Ritual and Belief* (London, 1914).

HAVEMEYER, L.: *The Drama of Savage Peoples* (Oxford, 1916).

MACGOWAN, K., AND ROSSE, H.: *Masks and Demons* (New York, 1923; London, 1924).

Masque, Le: Catalogue de l'Exposition du Musée royal des Beaux-Arts (Antwerp, 1956).

MORET, A.: *Mystères égyptiens* (New edition, Paris, 1927).

OESTERLEY, W. O. E.: *The Sacred Dance* (Cambridge, 1923).

RAGLAN, LORD: *The Hero* (London, 1936).

RIDGEWAY, W.: *The Dramas and Dramatic Dances of Non-European Races* (Cambridge, 1915).

RILEY, O. L.: *Masks and Magic* (New York, 1935).

SCHURÉ, E.: *The Genesis of Tragedy and the Sacred Drama of Eleusis* (London, 1936).

SETHE, K.: *Dramatische Texte zu altaegyptischen Mysterienspielen* (Leipzig, 1928).
SPENCE, LEWIS: *Myth and Ritual in Dance, Game and Rhyme* (London, 1947).
WEEGE, F.: *Der Tanz in der Antike* (Halle, 1926).

2: COSTUME IN THE GREEK AND ROMAN THEATRE

BIEBER, M.: *Das Dresdner Schauspielerrelief. Ein Beitrag zur Geschichte des tragischen Costüms in der griechischen Kunst* (Bonn, 1907).
—— *The History of the Greek and Roman Theater* (Princeton, 1939).
CORNFORD, F. M.: *The Origin of Attic Comedy* (London, 1914).
DIETERICH, A.: *Pulcinella, pompejanische Wandbilder und römische Satyrspiele* (Leipzig, 1897).
FLICKINGER, R. C.: *The Greek Theater and its Drama* (Chicago and Cambridge, 1918).
NICOLL, ALLARDYCE: *Masks, Mimes, and Miracles* (London, 1931).
SAUNDERS, C.: *Costume in Roman Comedy* (New York, 1909).
SÉCHAN, L.: *Études sur la tragédie grecque dans ses rapports avec la céramique* (Paris, 1927).

3: MYSTERIES, MIRACLES, AND MORALITIES

CRAIG, H.: *English Religious Drama of the Middle Ages* (Oxford, 1955).
GAYLEY, C. M.: *Plays of our Forefathers* (London, 1909).
KERNODLE, G. R.: *From Art to Theater* (Chicago, 1944).
MÂLE, É.: *L'Art religieux du XIIe au XVIIIe siècle* (Paris, 1946).
—— "Le Drame liturgique et l'iconographie de la Résurrection" (*Revue de l'Art*).
NICOLL, ALLARDYCE: *Masks, Mimes, and Miracles* (London, 1931).
PETIT DE JULLEVILLE, L.: *Les Mystères* (2 vols., Paris, 1880–86).
POLLARD, A. W.: *English Miracle Plays, Moralities and Interludes* (Oxford, 1904).
SHARP, T. A.: *A Dissertation on the Pageants or Dramatic Mysteries, anciently performed at Coventry* (Coventry, 1825).
YOUNG, K.: *The Drama of the Medieval Church* (2 vols., Oxford, 1933).

4: PAGEANT AND MASQUE BEGET OPERA AND BALLET

CHARTROU, J.: *Les Entrées solennelles et triomphales à la Renaissance (1484–1551)* (Paris, 1928).
DACIER, E.: "Les Scènes et figures théâtrales de Claude Gillot" (*Revue de l'Art*, xlv, 1924).

FISCHER, CARLOS: *Les Costumes de l'opéra* (Paris, 1931).

GREEN, A. W.: *The Inns of Court and Early English Drama* (New Haven and Oxford, 1931).

GREGOR, J.: *Monumenta Scenica* (Vienna and Munich, 1925–30).

MENÉSTRIER, C. F.: *Traité des tournois, ioustes, carousels, et autres spectacles publics* (Lyons, 1669).

NICOLL, ALLARDYCE: *Stuart Masques and the Renaissance Stage* (London, 1937; New York, 1938).

PRUNIÈRES, H.: *Le Ballet de cour en France avant Benserade et Lulli* (Paris, 1914).

SIMPSON, P., AND BELL, C. F.: *Designs by Inigo Jones for Masques and Plays at Court* (Walpole Society, vol. xii, Oxford, 1924).

WARBURG, A.: *I costumi teatrali per gli intermezzi del 1589* (Florence, 1895).

WELSFORD, ENID: *The Court Masque* (Cambridge, 1927).

5: THE COMMEDIA DELL'ARTE

ALBERT, M.: *Les Théâtres de la foire (1660–1789)* (Paris, 1900).

ANNUNZIO, G. D', AND BRUNELLESCHI, V.: *Les Masques et les personnages de la comédie italienne* (Paris, 1914).

BEAUMONT, C. W.: *The History of Harlequin* (London, 1926).

BROADBENT, R.: *A History of Pantomime* (London, 1901).

CELLER, L. (Leclerc): *Les Décors, les costumes et la mise-en-scène au XVIIe siècle (1615–80)* (Paris, 1860).

DISHER, M. WILLSON: *Clowns and Pantomimes* (London, 1925).

DUCHARTRE, P.-L.: *The Italian Comedy* (London, 1929).

SAND, M.: *Masques et bouffons (comédie italienne)* (2 vols., Paris, 1859).

SMITH, W.: *The Commedia dell'Arte* (New York and London, 1912).

6: COSTUME IN SHAKESPEARE'S PLAYS

BRADBROOK, M. C.: *Elizabethan Stage Conditions* (Cambridge, 1932).

CHAMBERS, SIR E. K.: *The Elizabethan Stage* (4 vols., Oxford, 1923).

ISAACS, J.: *Shakespeare in the Theatre* (Oxford, 1927).

KERNODLE, G. R.: *From Art to Theater* (Chicago, 1944).

LINTHICUM, M. C.: *Costume in the Drama of Shakespeare and his Contemporaries* (Oxford, 1936).

MERCHANT, W. M.: *Shakespeare and the Artist* (London, 1959).

THORNDIKE, A. H.: *Shakespeare's Theater* (New York and London, 1916).

7: OPERA AND BALLET

BEAUMONT, C. W.: *Five Centuries of Ballet Design* (London, 1939).

DACIER, E.: "Les Scènes et figures thèâtrales de Claude Gillot" (*Revue de l'Art*, xlv, 1924).

FISCHER, CARLOS: *Les Costumes de l'opéra* (Paris, 1931).

KOCHNO, B.: *Le Ballet* (Paris, 1954).

NUITTER, C.: *Costumes de l'Opéra, XVIIe et XVIIIe siècles* (Paris, 1883).

—— *Costumes des Ballets du Roy* (Paris, 1885).

PRUNIÈRES, H.: *Le Ballet de cour en France* (Paris, 1914).

TESSIER, A.: *Les Habits d'Opéra au XVIIIe siècle.*

8: FROM NOVERRE TO DIAGHILEV

FISCHER, CARLOS: *Les Costumes de l'opéra* (Paris, 1931).

NICOLL, ALLARDYCE: *The Development of the Theatre* (fourth edition, London, 1958).

9: THE TWENTIETH CENTURY

ALEXANDRE, A.: *The Decorative Art of Léon Bakst* (London, 1913).

BRAGAGLIA, A. G.: *Del Teatro teatrale* (Rome, 1929).

CARTER, HUNTLY: *The Theatre of Max Reinhardt* (London, 1914).

—— *The New Spirit in the European Theatre 1914–1924* (London, 1925).

CHENEY, SHELDON: *The New Movement in the Theater* (New York, 1914).

GREGOR, J., AND FÜLOP-MILLER: *Das amerikanische Theater und Kino* (Vienna, 1931).

——*Das russische Theater* (Vienna, 1927).

GRUBE, M.: *Geschichte der Meininger* (Berlin, 1926).

KOMISARJEVSKY, T., AND SIMONSON, L.: *Settings and Costumes of the Modern Stage* (London, 1933).

LAVER, J.: *Stage Designs and Costumes by Oliver Messel* (London, 1933).

MOUSSINAC, L.: *Tendances nouvelles du théâtre* (Paris, 1931).

PLAYFAIR, NIGEL: *The Story of the Lyric Theatre, Hammersmith* (London, 1925).

PROPERT, W. A.: *The Russian Ballet in Western Europe (1909–1920)* (London, 1921).

SAYLER, O. M.: *The Russian Theatre under the Revolution* (1920).

—— (editor): *Max Reinhardt and his Theatre* (New York and London, 1924).

SHERINGHAM, G., AND LAVER, J.: *Design in the Theatre* (London, 1927).

STERN, E., AND HERALD, H. (editors): *Reinhardt und seine Bühne* (Berlin, 1918).

Victoria and Albert Museum, London. Catalogue and Bibliography, International Theatre Exhibition (1922).